RECREATING HUMANITY

Illuminating Our Divine Identity in Christ

SAMEH SAIED

LOGOS ECHOES

Contents

Preface
Introduction

Chapter One.
Restoring the Divine Image:
From Fall to Spiritual Renewal.

Chapter Two.
The Body and Spirit in the New Creation of Humanity

Chapter Three.
Divine Design:
From Creation to Redemption and Resurrection

Chapter Four.
Eternal Transformation:
Embracing the New Creation and Its Good Works.

Chapter Five.
Baptism and the New Creation:
Unveiling Transformation and Son-ship

Chapter Seven.
The New Self in Christ :
Defining Traits and the Return to a New Heart

Chapter Eight.
Eternal Life Unveiled:
Faith, Love, and the New Creation in Christ

Chapter Nine.
Standing Before God :
The New Creation Through Worship and Prayer.

Epilogue

The Pinnacle of the New Creation Intended by God for
Humanity

About LOGOS ECHOES Publications
About the Author

Yet to all who did receive him,
to those who believed in his name,
he gave the right to become children of
God,
children born not of natural descent, nor
of human decision or a husband's will,
but born of God

John 1:12-13

The New Creation:
The Divine Purpose of Christ's Incarnation, Death, and Resurrection

When discussing the birth, death, and resurrection of Christ, we are not just recounting historical events but exploring profound truths that impact us deeply. Theologically, the birth of Christ signifies that the Word, the Son of God, took on human flesh from the Virgin Mary. She was chosen as a pure and sacred vessel, embodying the highest ideals of humanity. Through the Holy Spirit, it was made clear that the child born of her was indeed the *"Son of God,"* as the angel declared.

The Word, being infinite and boundless, united with human flesh in a way that transcends mere human limitations. When Christ assumed human form from the Virgin Mary, this body gained divine attributes, reflecting the infinite nature of the Son of God. This unity signifies that the body Christ took on was not just an individual body but a vessel that embraced all of humanity.

Thus, when Christ was crucified while bearing our sins, the Apostle Paul explains that we were spiritually crucified with Him. When He died, we all died with Him; when He rose, we all rose with Him; and when He ascended into heaven, we were spiritually seated with Him in the heavenly realms. This mystery of the Incarnation means that the divine nature of Christ merged with human nature, creating a single, unified nature — one person with both divine and human qualities—without mixing, separation, or alteration.

Through His miraculous birth, Christ took on all of humanity within Himself, encompassing us through His suffering, death, and resurrection. We were all spiritually crucified with Him.

Because He bore the punishment that was rightfully ours. As the Holy and Sinless One, He did not deserve these sufferings; they were ours due to the inherited curse and eternal death from Adam.

Christ's death and resurrection lifted this curse from us. As Paul writes: "*But God, who is rich in mercy, because of His great love with which He loved us, even when we were dead in trespasses, made us alive together with Christ—by grace you have been saved—and raised us up together, and made us sit together in the heavenly places in Christ Jesus*" (Eph.2:4-6). This signifies our transition from a state of death in sin to a state of life in righteousness through Christ. It is the essence of our faith and the source of our hope—a free gift we must accept with gratitude and confidence. As Scripture says: "*That in the ages to come He might show the exceeding riches of His grace in His kindness toward us in Christ Jesus. For by grace you have been saved through faith, and that not of yourselves; it is the gift of God, not of works, lest anyone should boast*" (Eph.2:7-9).

The Apostle Paul further explains: "*If one died for all, then all died*" (2 Cor.5:14). This illustrates that Christ is not merely an individual; He embodies the divine nature that imparts completeness to His human body. Hence, all who believe in Christ have spiritually died and risen with Him, fulfilling Adam's penalty and being freed from sin, thereby receiving the resurrection that defines the new humanity in Christ. As Paul notes: "*We have been crucified with Christ... and raised with Him*" (Eph.2:5-6).

Paul clarifies this by saying: "*Because of His great love with which He loved us and 'according to the riches of His mercy.'*" Those who were considered dead in eternal death due to sins have been made alive with Christ through faith — a gift from God, not from ourselves. We now live with Christ in eternal life and resurrection as a new creation, having overcome death and sin with Him. This is our Christian faith, which, when embraced with confidence, infuses us with the spirit of the new humanity, empowering us to act and testify to God's love and grace.

INTRODUCTION

In exploring Christ's conversation with Nicodemus, we encounter one of the deepest mysteries of Christian faith: the concept of the second birth, also known as the *"new creation."* Have you ever considered that this notion might be more than just spiritual renewal? It could signify a profound call to transform the world at its very roots and initiate a fundamental change in our understanding of ourselves and humanity. Picture yourself on the edge of a vast chasm, observing various realms where conflicting beliefs and philosophies are in turmoil. Amid escalating crises and conflicts, millions wonder: how can humanity find light in the darkness? If there is an answer, it might lie in the *"new creation"* that Christianity presents as a means to renew humanity from its core. This idea is not just a religious concept; it is an invitation to fundamentally reshape everything—to undergo a radical shift in our approach to life and embrace new values. The path to this new birth is not about mere wishes or hopes but involves a profound transformation that redefines the essence of what it means to be human. Christ's discussion of the *"new creation"* is not merely a historical account or philosophical analysis; it is a profound exploration of spiritual renewal's power and a reflection on humanity's potential to rise above its weaknesses and failures to create a new, hopeful, and inspiring future.

To understand what the new creation entails, as Christianity describes it, we look to Nicodemus, who grappled with this question on our behalf. He approached Jesus with a mixture of fear and doubt, asking a crucial question: How can one enter the Kingdom of God, and who is worthy of this supreme honour? Jesus answered, "*Very truly I tell you, no one can see the Kingdom of God unless they are born again*" (John.3:3). Nicodemus struggled to grasp this concept, focusing on the term "*born again*," and asked in confusion: "*How can someone be born when they are old? Surely they cannot enter a second time into their mother's womb to be born!*" (John.3:4). Understanding the difficulty this idea posed for Nicodemus, Jesus explained: "*Very truly I tell you, no one can enter the Kingdom of God unless they are born of water and the Spirit*" (John.3:5). To clarify and prevent Nicodemus from thinking of a physical rebirth, Jesus said: "*Flesh gives birth to flesh, but the Spirit gives birth to spirit*" (John.3:6). This meant that the second birth is a spiritual rebirth, distinct from physical birth. To further address Nicodemus's confusion, Jesus added: "*You should not be surprised at my saying, 'You must be born again.' The wind blows wherever it pleases. You hear its sound, but you cannot tell where it comes from or where it is going*" (John.3:7-8). Jesus aimed to communicate that the second birth from above, achieved through water and the Spirit—baptism—is a supernatural process, resulting in a spiritual rebirth on earth, with a mystery that transcends human understanding. Thus, Nicodemus learned that this new birth from above involves a process on earth through water and the Spirit, enveloped in an ineffable mystery.

At the core of Christ's mission lies the profound concept of the second birth, also known as the "*new creation.*" This idea extends far beyond mere spiritual renewal, suggesting a radical transformation designed to fundamentally reshape humanity. By uniting with human nature through His incarnation from the Virgin Mary and the Holy Spirit, Christ established a path for humanity to journey with Him from the beginning of time to its ultimate fulfilment. His birth was marked by the angelic proclamation of *"Glory to God in the highest, and on earth peace,"* signifying the manifestation of divine glory and the establishment of peace for humanity. This event symbolized the replacement of historical enmity and sorrow with divine joy and reconciliation.

Christ's birth, thus, represents the first glimpse of the new human being born from above. This new creation is not merely a symbolic idea but the first tangible expression of a transformation that would reshape human existence. As we follow Christ through His earthly life, His sacrificial death, and His triumphant resurrection, we witness the unfolding of this new creation. His resurrection signifies the first instance of humanity's transformation from the curse of eternal death that had plagued Adam and his descendants. Christ's resurrection stands as the initial manifestation of this new spiritual creation, with Saint Paul referring to Him as the *"firstborn from the dead"*—the pioneer of those who will rise from the dead.

In our resurrection with Christ, we are presented to God the Father as a new creation. This transformation is not merely about physical resurrection but a profound renewal of the spirit. Christ's ascension to the heavens and His position at the Father's right hand with His glorified body symbolize the inauguration of the Kingdom of God, bringing with Him the redeemed new humanity. This pivotal moment in Christian theology demonstrates how Christ has opened the way for humanity to enter into the divine realm, establishing a new relationship between God and humankind.

The concept of the *"new creation"* or the second birth from above, through water and the Spirit, is not an afterthought but a central element of God's eternal plan. This plan was chosen in Christ before the world's foundation, and it underpins the essence of prophetic messages, the person of Christ, the Gospel, and the Kingdom of God. It embodies the divine intention to transform humanity fundamentally.

For some, the idea of the "*new creation*" might be familiar, while for others it may be new, but it remains an essential aspect of Christian faith and personal relationship with Christ. This concept offers a fresh and profound perspective on human renewal, highlighting its critical role in our spiritual lives and our interaction with the world. The new creation is not just a theological concept but a practical guide for living out Christian values in a complex world.

Today, our world is fraught with challenges and crises that profoundly impact human nature and daily existence. We are confronted with a multitude of intellectual and moral currents that challenge fundamental humanitarian principles while other movements strive to address the flaws in our nature. The rise in global conflict, injustice, and animosity makes the need for personal and internal renewal more urgent than ever.

In this tumultuous environment, if we place our faith in Jesus Christ, the Bible offers us a compass to navigate these difficulties. As Scripture instructs, "*Since then, you have been raised with Christ, set your hearts on things above, where Christ is, seated at the right hand of God*" (Col.3:1). Christian faith transcends being merely a set of beliefs; it is a dynamic and living call to transform our lives according to divine principles of truth, justice, and love.

Our aim is to explore how the Christian perspective on human renewal can influence our daily lives and act as a powerful force for positive change. As Paul the Apostle notes, "*For if we have been united with Him in a death like His, we will certainly also be united with Him in a resurrection like*

His" (Rom.6:4). By deeply engaging with biblical teachings, we will uncover how to live lives marked by inner peace and promote social justice. This approach not only contributes to the expansion of God's Kingdom on earth but also enriches our personal spiritual journey.

We will also examine how faith in Christ can inspire and motivate us to address the current world's challenges and how we can become agents of genuine renewal in a world shrouded in darkness. As the Bible highlights, *"No one can redeem the life of another or give to God a ransom for them"* (Ps.49:7). This principle underscores the importance of applying Christian values in practical ways, helping us navigate difficulties and crises effectively.

Our goal extends beyond providing a theoretical analysis of human renewal. We aim to offer practical, actionable guidance that enhances our relationship with God, fosters genuine personal transformation, and actively contributes to building a better world. We believe that biblical teachings offer the necessary roadmap to navigate life's storms, and our spiritual journey can serve as a source of hope and change for both ourselves and the broader world. As Scripture encourages, *"Let us not become weary in doing good, for at the proper time we will reap a harvest if we do not give up"* (Gal.6:9).

Let us embrace this exploration with courage and faith, striving to make our world a brighter and more compassionate place. We should remain ever ready for the Lord's return and committed to demonstrating His love and mercy in every aspect of our lives. Through this commitment, we can contribute to a transformative renewal that not only impacts our personal lives but also extends to the world around us.

This book offers a comprehensive examination of this transformative doctrine, structured around a series of profound insights into the nature of our new identity in Christ.

Chapter One: *"Restoring the Divine Image: From Fall to Spiritual Renewal"*, begins by reflecting on the creation and fall of humanity, setting the stage for our understanding of the divine image and human experience. We will delve into God's plan for humanity's renewal, unravel the distortion of our original divine image, and explore the path to spiritual renewal. This chapter establishes the foundational understanding of our transformation from the fall to redemption.

Chapter Two: *"The Body and Spirit in the New Creation of Humanity"*, explores the profound interplay between body and spirit in the new creation. It examines the purpose behind humanity's creation, the struggle between flesh and spirit, and the assurance of grace and redemption. We will also investigate the sources of conflict between flesh and spirit, the nature of the new man, and his role in the kingdom. The chapter concludes with a discussion on the new body and judgment, illuminating how our new creation impacts our physical and spiritual existence.

Chapter Three:*" Divine Design: From Creation to Redemption and Resurrection"*, expands our perspective to encompass the divine plan from the first creation to the resurrection. We will delve into the nature of Christ's redemption and understand the atonement, as well as the revelation and fulfilment of the new resurrected body. This chapter offers a comprehensive view of how divine design unfolds from creation through to redemption and resurrection.

Chapter Four: *"Eternal Transformation: Embracing the New Creation and Its Good Works"*, focuses on how we live out the new creation through good works. We will explore the resurrection of Christ as the revelation of the new creation, the essential path of good works reflecting Christ's mission, and what constitutes good works in the new creation. Additionally, we will examine the nature and foundation of these good works, and how they are rooted in Christ Jesus.

Chapter Five: *"Baptism and the New Creation: Unveiling Transformation and Son-ship"*, addresses the role of baptism as the gateway to the new creation. This chapter discusses baptism as the mystical death of the old self, the revelation of son-ship to the new man, and how the new self is freed from sin and judgment. It also explores the relationship between baptism and the cross, and the awareness of the new man rooted in faith, hope, and love.

Chapter Six: *"The New Baptismal Identity: Revealing the Resurrection and Redemption"*, examines our new identity in Christ through baptism. We will discuss the new baptismal man, the church, and the body of Christ, and how the resurrection image of Christ is reflected in our new bodies. The chapter concludes with an exploration of redemption through Christ's suffering and resurrection.

Chapter Seven: *"The New Self in Christ: Defining Traits and the Return to a New Heart"*, provides an in-depth look at the characteristics of the new self. We will explore how to embrace the new self, identify its defining traits, and discuss the return to a new heart, highlighting the transformative power of Christ.

Chapter Eight: *"Eternal Life Unveiled: Faith, Love, and the New Creation in Christ"*, delves into the concepts of faith, love, and eternal life in relation to our new creation. This chapter covers faith in Christ and personal relationship with Him, the revelation of Christ and the promise of eternal life, and the Apostle John's teachings on sin, atonement, and eternal life. It also explores love, knowledge, and revelation as they pertain to understanding eternal life and embracing our new creation.

Chapter Nine: *"Standing Before God: The New Creation Through Worship and Prayer"*, addresses the practical implications of the new creation in our worship and prayer life. We will discuss the essence of standing before God, the divine invitation to worship in spirit and truth, and the urgency of prayer as demonstrated by Christ. The chapter emphasizes the sanctity of love and the requirements for standing before God.

This book aims to guide readers through a profound understanding of how the new creation redefines our existence, our relationships with God and each other, and our spiritual journey. Through detailed scriptural study and theological reflection, we seek to illuminate the path from our fallen state to the glorious new creation envisioned by God.

CHAPTER ONE.

RESTORING THE DIVINE IMAGE:
FROM FALL TO SPIRITUAL RENEWAL.

The Creation and Fall of Humanity: A Reflection on Divine Image and Human Experience

When we delve into the Book of Genesis, we encounter the profound origins of humanity: *"Then God said, 'Let Us make man in Our image, according to Our likeness...' So God created man in His own image; in the image of God He created him; male and female He created them. Then God blessed them and said to them, 'Be fruitful and multiply; fill the earth and subdue it; have dominion'"* (Gen.1:26-28).

Additionally, Genesis describes: *"And the Lord God formed man of the dust of the ground, and breathed into his nostrils the breath of life; and man became a living being"* (Gen.2:7). *"And the Lord God said, 'It is not good that man should be alone; I will make him a helper comparable to him...' So the Lord God caused a deep sleep to fall on Adam, and he slept; then He took one of his ribs and closed up the flesh in its place. And the rib which the Lord God had taken from man He made into a woman; and He brought her to the man. And Adam said, 'This is now bone of my bones and flesh of my flesh; she shall be called Woman, because she was taken out of Man'"* (Gen.2:18, 21-23).

What stands out in this account is that humanity was initially created from the dust of the earth. God breathed life into this form, making Adam a living soul. Thus, Adam represents the integration of both earthly matter and divine spirit. Essentially, humanity is a union of body and spirit. The body, made from earthly dust, is temporary, whereas the spirit, which comes from God, is eternal and more significant.

The soul or spirit, created in God's image, initially reflected divine likeness. However, after the fall of Adam and the subsequent curse, this divine image became distorted, and the resemblance to God was lost. The soul, once in perfect alignment with God's image, now bore the marks of this corruption.

The relationship between the body, formed from the earth, and the soul, created in God's image, can be understood as an impression of the original essence. The body was meant to reflect the soul's divine nature. According to parapsychology, when the soul departs from the body, it retains an accurate reflection of the person's essence, which is considered the true core of creation. Scientists refer to this essence as the archetype, while the body is seen as the outward image. While the image is transient, the essence remains enduring.

However, with Adam's fall, this divine image within the soul was fractured, leading to a distortion of the original impression. The human body no longer reflected the divine attributes of glory, wisdom, majesty, and holiness. This fall led to a profound rupture in the relationship with God, resulting in a loss of love, intimacy, and obedience, as well as wisdom, sanctity, and righteousness. Humanity found itself estranged, isolated, and desolate, grappling with the realities of sin, disobedience, and separation from God.

Restoring the Divine Image (1): God's Plan for Humanity's Renewal

From the beginning, God created humanity to be His beloved and cherished friends, designed to worship and glorify Him eternally. However, when Adam fell and was banished from God's presence, returning to the earth from which he was formed—*"for dust you are, and to dust you shall return"* (Gen.3:19)—God set out to restore His original plan. He initiated a process to bring about a new creation, a second birth, based on a foundation that would not be subject to death, disobedience, or separation. This time, God intended to create humanity not only in His image but through the Spirit and resurrected body of His Son. The new creation would come from the divine righteousness and holiness of Christ, rather than from the earthly dust, enabling humanity to live before God in purity, without fault, and to praise His grace forever.

Saint Paul, through divine revelation, discovered that this spiritual creation, designed to mirror the resurrected Son, was part of God's plan even before the physical world was created. The creation of humanity from dust was not a mistake but a preliminary stage in God's grand design. This initial stage allowed humanity to evolve from a material to a spiritual creation, moving from weakness and corruption to perfection and righteousness, reflecting God's practice of starting from simplicity and achieving ultimate excellence.

Paul writes: *"Blessed be the God and Father of our Lord Jesus Christ, who has blessed us with every spiritual blessing in the heavenly places in Christ. Just as He chose us in Him before the foundation of the world, that we should be holy and without blame before Him in love, having predestined us to adoption as sons by Jesus Christ to Himself, according to the good pleasure of His will, to the praise of the glory of His grace, by which He made us accepted in the Beloved"* (Eph.1:3-6). This passage highlights that our election and predestination in Christ occurred before the world was formed, affirming that this spiritual creation precedes and surpasses the earthly creation.

The terms *"blessed us in Christ," "chosen us in Christ before the foundation of the world,"* and *"predestined us for adoption by Jesus Christ"* all refer to the ultimate divine plan for humanity's spiritual creation, distinct from our physical origins. Our complete and final spiritual creation, established by God before the creation of the world, is closely connected with Christ, the Son and the Word. This plan existed before time and the world itself. Therefore, the spiritual creation of humanity is higher and more significant than any other creation, being part of God's original design before the world was established.

But ,What does it mean to be *"blessed in Christ," "chosen in Christ,"* and *"predestined for adoption through Christ before the foundation of the world"*? Christ is known as the *"Word"* and Son of God before the world's foundation. This indicates that the creation of humanity in God's image and likeness, as described in Genesis—*"Let Us make man in Our image, according to Our likeness"*—means humanity was created in the image of the Son of God. Paul affirms this by stating that *"God predestined us to adoption as sons by Jesus Christ"* (Eph.1:5). Thus, humanity was created, according to God's plan, to be children of God in the Son and to reflect the Son's righteousness and holiness. Paul further explains that *"He predestined them to be conformed to the image of His Son"* (Rom. 8:29).

This concept pertains to the spirit of humanity rather than the earthly body, which entered the world as a lower stage in human creation and must be transcended for the full revelation of the new spiritual creation. When Christ, the Son of God in the flesh, came to announce the Kingdom of God — humanity's true spiritual home — He also revealed the necessity of a new creation from the Son's nature, exemplified by His resurrection, to qualify humanity for entry into the Kingdom of God. Christ referred to this new spiritual creation as a *"new birth"* or *"birth from above,"* stating, *"Most assuredly, I say to you, unless one is born again, he cannot see the kingdom of God"* (John.3:3). He further clarified: *"Most assuredly, I say to you, unless one is born of water and the Spirit, he cannot enter the kingdom of God. That which is born of the flesh is flesh, and that which is born of the Spirit is spirit"* (John.3:5-6).

To achieve this new birth from above, the Word, the Son of God, took on human form — one that had become corrupted and distorted from its original state. His purpose was to restore humanity to its original glory. This restoration ensures that sin and death no longer affect humanity, and the earthly body, which contributed to the flaws in the initial creation, is set aside, given the curse: *"For dust you are, and to dust you shall return"* (Gen. 3:19).

Restoring the Divine Image (2): Understanding the Distortion of Humanity

To begin with, we must explore the nature of the distortion that has affected the divine image and likeness in humanity. Originally, the human body was created to be incorruptible. Sin did not originate from the body itself; rather, it resulted from the misuse of human free will and knowledge. As a creation of God, the body itself cannot be inherently sinful or flawed. The human body was designed to be pure and perfect, but the freedom of human will allowed for the possibility of disobedience.

When Satan tempted Adam and Eve to act against God's will and guidance, the essential connection between divine will and human will was severed. As a result, Adam lost his inherent protection and righteousness, leaving him exposed and flawed. This rupture of the divine image and distortion of the likeness made him unfit to remain in God's presence, leading to his expulsion and separation from divine life.

So, how can the divine image be restored and the likeness be realigned? The core issue was the disconnection between human free will and knowledge and the divine will and knowledge. Humanity's inability to recognize or pursue the truth stemmed from this separation. Paul describes this state of humanity before Christ's redemption: *"For I do not understand my own actions. For I do not do what I want, but I do the very thing I hate... For I have the desire to do what is right, but not the ability to carry it out... For I do not do the good I want, but the evil I do not want is what I keep on doing"* (Rom.7:15, 18, 19).

In this condition, humanity fell into bondage to sin and Satan, having lost its connection with God at the levels of will and knowledge. The body became a tool for sin rather than a vessel of divine purpose. To restore humanity, God needed to create a new spiritual existence aligned with His divine nature. This renewal involved creating a new being from the nature of Christ, ensuring that this new creation would fully embody God's will, desire, and understanding.

As Paul writes, humanity is called to understand *"the depths of God"*: *"But, as it is written, 'What no eye has seen, nor ear heard, nor the heart of man imagined, what God has prepared for those who love Him' — these things God has revealed to us through the Spirit. For the Spirit searches everything, even the depths of God"* (1 Cor.2:9-10). Furthermore, Paul describes the goal of being filled with the fullness of God: *"And to know the love of Christ that surpasses knowledge, that you may be filled with all the fullness of God"* (Eph.3:19). This encapsulates the profound spiritual renewal that aligns humanity once more with the divine image and purpose.

Restoring the Divine Image (3): The Path to Spiritual Renewal

To restore humanity to its original divine image and likeness, God first needed to lift the penalty of eternal death and the curse that had resulted in separation from Him. This separation made it impossible for humanity to reconnect with God through its own flawed capabilities. Therefore, it was necessary for the Son of God to take on human form — without sin. He assumed a pure and holy body from the Virgin Mary through the Holy Spirit, then took upon Himself the sins of humanity. He was judged as a sinner, did not defend Himself, and accepted the penalty of sin, including suffering and death. By doing so, He fulfilled the penalty for sin in the human body.

When Jesus was crucified, He also bore the curse, thereby redeeming the body from punishment and curse by fulfilling them on our behalf. Consequently, death could not hold Him, and He triumphed over it because His death completely addressed the penalty for sin. His resurrection defeated death. In this way, by His death and resurrection, Christ created a new spiritual body for humanity, one that is incapable of sinning, as John writes: *"No one born of God makes a practice of sinning, for God's seed abides in him; and he cannot keep on sinning because he has been born of God"* (1 John.3:9).

The resurrected body of Christ was a spiritual body, retaining all natural human characteristics except for sin, and thus exempt from death. This resurrected body, granted to us through the sacrament of baptism, is described by Paul: *"For as many of you as were baptized into Christ have put on Christ"* (Gal.3:27). This new spiritual body, created by Christ, is imparted to us through baptism, symbolizing our new identity in Him. Thus, Paul affirms, *"For we are his workmanship, created in Christ Jesus for good works, which God prepared beforehand, that we should walk in them"* (Eph.2:10) and *"so that he might create in himself one new man in place of the two, so making peace"* (Eph.2:15).

Baptism represents the mystery of new creation through water and the Spirit, as Jesus said. This new creation is formed in Christ through a profound union, endowing us with His attributes: *"And put on the new self, created after the likeness of God in true righteousness and holiness"* (Eph.4:24). In baptism, Christ imparts His resurrected nature to us, overcoming sin and death, while putting to death the old body crucified on the cross: *"We know that our old self was crucified with him in order that the body of sin might be brought to nothing, so that we would no longer be enslaved to sin"* (Rom.6:6). *"If Christ is in you, although the body is dead because of sin, the Spirit is life because of righteousness"* (Rom 8:10).

This transformation occurs in baptism, where we participate in Christ's death and resurrection through faith: *"You have put off the old self with its practices and have put on the new self, which is being renewed in knowledge after the image of its creator"* (Colo.3:9-10). Through what Christ accomplished on the cross and bestowed upon us in baptism — both the death of the old self and the resurrection of the new spiritual self — Christ has restored the divine image and likeness in us. This new self, which cannot sin because it is of the nature of the resurrected Christ, fulfils the promise of eternal life: *"Everyone who has been born of God does not sin, because His seed remains in him; and he cannot sin, because he has been born of God"* (1 John.3:9). Thus, humanity is officially qualified for the inheritance of eternal life through adoption, secured by union with Christ, the Son of God: *"The Spirit himself bears witness with our spirit that we are children of God, and if children, then heirs — heirs of God and fellow heirs with Christ"* (Rom.8:16-17).

Ultimately, we must firmly believe that no teaching, whether old or new, can convince us to deny or undervalue the nature of the new self-created in Christ. This new nature, inherited through His resurrection, is not merely a set of attributes or gifts but a created essence: *"the new self, created after the likeness of God in true righteousness and holiness"* (Eph.4:24). It is realized as Christ Himself is formed within us: *"My little children, for whom I am again in the anguish of childbirth until Christ is formed in you"* (Gal.4:19).

CHAPTER TWO.
THE BODY AND SPIRIT IN THE NEW CREATION OF HUMANITY.

Rebirth from the Spirit as the Path to Divine Restoration

Christ Himself first articulated the concept of dual birth within Christian faith during His conversation with Nicodemus, a member of the Jewish Sanhedrin. He explained the necessity of a new birth to see and enter the Kingdom of God. He said, *"Very truly I tell you, no one can see the Kingdom of God unless they are born again"* (John.3:3). To clarify how this rebirth occurs, He added, *"Very truly I tell you, no one can enter the Kingdom of God unless they are born of water and the Spirit"* (John.3:5). This indicates that to enter the divine realm of God's Kingdom, one must undergo a spiritual rebirth, signifying a profound, heavenly transformation.

Christ then differentiated between being born of the flesh and being born of the Spirit. He stated, *"Flesh gives birth to flesh, but the Spirit gives birth to spirit"* (John.3:6). By introducing this concept, Christ offered ordinary, sinful humanity the opportunity for a second, spiritual birth. Thus, a person born of the flesh could also be born of the Spirit, acquiring a new, spiritual nature.

So, Why did Christ provide this second birth from the Spirit? Initially, humans were created from dust and given life through God's breath. They were earthly beings with a divine image, possessing knowledge and free will. However, they misused these gifts, disobeying God and indulging in forbidden actions. This misuse led to a distortion of their knowledge and a loss of control over their will, resulting in their descent into earthly desires.

Humanity became vulnerable to the devil, who tempted Eve in the Garden of Eden. The serpent questioned Eve, *"Did God really say, 'You must not eat from any tree in the garden'?"* (Gen.3:1). Acting on her own understanding, Eve responded with falsehood: *"We may eat fruit from the trees in the garden, but God said, 'You shall not eat fruit from the tree that is in the midst of the garden, nor shall you touch it, lest you die'"* (Gen.3:2-3). The serpent then deceived her with poisoned truth, saying, *"You will not certainly die. For God knows that when you eat from it your eyes will be opened, and you will be like God, knowing good and evil"* (Gen. 3:4-5). While this statement contained partial truth, it was laced with deception.

God granted humanity freedom and knowledge, but these gifts were intended to be exercised within divine boundaries, with knowledge derived from God's guidance. Disobedience severed this connection, leaving humanity's freedom unprotected and subject to the devil's influence. Eve failed to recognize the trap in the serpent's seemingly true words, leading to her fall. The text tells us, *"When the woman saw that the fruit of the tree was good for food and pleasing to the eye—and also desirable for gaining wisdom—she took some and ate it. She also gave some to her husband, who was with her, and he ate it. Then the eyes of both of them were opened, and they realized they were naked"* (Gen.3:6-7). This act of disobedience led to Adam's fall and the loss of divine protection and guidance.

Thus, humanity in its earthly form lost its safeguarded freedom and truth. Though it retained free will and knowledge, it could no longer maintain freedom from the devil's control nor recognize the truth that preserves it from sin.

Given this situation, what could God do for humanity, which had succumbed to earthly desires and lost its knowledge of the divine? The only solution was for humanity to undergo a new creation, not from dust but from the Spirit. This new creation was necessary to restore what was lost and bring humanity back into alignment with divine truth and freedom.

The Purpose Behind Humanity's Creation: From Earthly Beginnings to Spiritual Renewal

The purpose of creating humanity from the dust of the earth was for God to have a being from the earth that would worship Him, live with Him, and be elevated to Him. However, when this initial creation failed due to its earthly nature, God decided to create humanity a new from the nature of His Son—an immortal, incorruptible, and spiritual essence. To achieve this, He sent His *"Word,"* embodying His thoughts, Son-ship, will, and actions.

God's intention was clear: He aimed to grant humanity His Word, which represents divine knowledge, to open human understanding to the knowledge of God. As Jesus stated, *"I have made you known to them, and will continue to make you known in order that the love you have for me may be in them and that I myself may be in them"* (John.17:26). Instead of the son-ship given to Adam, which became the source of sin, God intended to offer humanity the right of adoption, making God their Father: *"The Spirit himself testifies with our spirit that we are*

God's children" (Rom.8:16). In place of the freedom that Adam lost to Satan, God granted them *"the freedom and glory of the children of God"* (Rom.8:21), and Jesus affirmed, *"If the Son sets you free, you will be free indeed"* (John.8:36).

Thus, the *"Word"* of God, His Son, took on human flesh and assumed *"the likeness of sinful flesh"* (Rom.8:3), though He was without sin. This demonstrated that flesh itself is not inherently sinful. Sin arises from a will deprived of God's guidance and from incomplete knowledge corrupted by Satan. The incarnate Word, Jesus Christ, bore our sins in His body on the cross, becoming subject to death and punishment as a human, despite being sinless as God. By dying in the flesh, He completed the penalty, defeated death, and rose with the same flesh—our flesh—that was crucified. He rose without sin and in an imperishable state, granting us His resurrected body to become our new spiritual body. Christ thus became our new Father, the second Adam, and the Spirit from heaven, replacing the first earthly Adam. As Paul explains, *"The first man Adam became a living being; the last Adam, a life-giving spirit... The first man was of the dust of the earth; the second man is the Lord from heaven... And just as we have borne the image of the earthly man, so shall we bear the image of the heavenly man"* (1 Cor.15:45, 47, 49).

Christ has bestowed this spiritual body upon us through the sacrament of baptism, where we are reborn by the Spirit, becoming conformed to His image of righteousness and holiness. John writes, *"Yet to all who did receive him, to those who believed in his name, he gave the right to become children of God—children born not of natural descent, nor of human decision or a husband's will, but born of God"* (John.1:12-13). Paul further affirms this in several passages: *"He saved us, not because of righteous things we had done, but because of his mercy. He saved us through the washing of rebirth and renewal by the Holy Spirit"* (Titus.3:5); *"So in Christ Jesus you are all children of God through faith. For all of you who were baptized into Christ have clothed yourselves with Christ"* (Gal.3:26-27); and *"You were taught, with regard to your former way of life, to put off your old self, which is being corrupted by its deceitful desires; to be made new in the attitude of your minds; and to put on the new self, created to be like God in true righteousness and holiness"* (Eph.4:22-24). Peter confirms this truth: *"For you have been born again, not of perishable seed, but of imperishable, through the living and enduring word of God"* (1 Peter .1:23).

Thus, God has granted us a tremendous gift following our initial earthly creation: a new spiritual creation from above, through water and the Spirit, in the new humanity created in Christ and of His resurrected nature. This new creation is continually renewed in us by the Holy Spirit: *"We are being transformed into his image with ever-increasing glory, which comes from the Lord, who is the Spirit"* (2 Cor.3:18). Consequently, humanity now consists of two elements: the old sinful earthly self, doomed to death and prone to sin, and the new spiritual self from heaven, resembling Christ in His resurrected state. This new self is not governed by sin but by the law of the Spirit of life in Christ. It is not under the yoke of sin but under grace and the guidance of the Holy Spirit. John asserts that those who believe in Christ and are baptized are born of God into a new birth, are incapable of sinning, and are under the leadership of the Holy Spirit: *"No one born of God makes a practice of sinning, for God's seed abides in him, and he cannot keep on sinning because he has been born of God"* (1 John.3:9), and *"We know that anyone born of God does not sin, but the one born of God keeps him safe, and the evil one does not touch him"* (1 John.5:18).

The Struggle Between Flesh and Spirit: The Assurance of Grace and Redemption

In the struggle between living for Christ and God the Father, the Apostle Paul captures the conflict within us: *"For the flesh desires what is contrary to the Spirit, and the Spirit what is contrary to the flesh. They are in conflict with each other, so that you are not to do whatever you want"* (Gal.5:17). He further explains, *"If you live according to the flesh, you will die; but if by the Spirit you put to death the misdeeds of the body, you will live. For those who are led by the Spirit of God are the children of God"* (Rom.8:13-14).

Yet, Paul provides reassurance that the believer has the advantage. The new self is governed by grace and bound by the Spirit, rendering the old sinful nature ineffective. Paul asserts, *"For sin shall no longer be your master, because you are not under the law, but under grace"* (Rom.6:14). This indicates that while the old nature may still attempt to act on earthly desires, Paul emphasizes that *"the body is dead because of sin, yet the Spirit is life because of righteousness"* (Rom.8:10). This new life in the Spirit is rooted in Christ's resurrection. Paul also affirms that the blood of Christ has truly purified us from dead works, erasing them from our conscience: *"How much more, then, will the blood of Christ, who through the eternal Spirit offered himself unblemished to God, cleanse our consciences from acts that lead to death, so that we may serve the living God!"* (Heb.9:14).

The Apostle John further emphasizes this grace and our rightful claim to eternal life. He urges us to fully embrace the fellowship granted through the revelation of eternal life in the Father and in Christ, saying, *"We proclaim to you what we have seen and heard, so that you also may have fellowship with us.*

And our fellowship is with the Father and with his Son, Jesus Christ. We write this to make our joy complete" (1 John.1:3-4).

While this does not mean we are free from sin in the flesh, John assures us that these sins are covered by Christ's intercession and atonement: *"The blood of Jesus, his Son, purifies us from all sin. If we claim to be without sin, we deceive ourselves and the truth is not in us. If we confess our sins, he is faithful and just and will forgive us our sins and purify us from all unrighteousness"* (1 John.1:7-9). Furthermore, *"If anybody does sin, we have an advocate with the Father—Jesus Christ, the Righteous One. He is the atoning sacrifice for our sins"* (1 John.2:1-2).

From John's writings and his message, it is clear that we are meant to experience the eternal life revealed through Christ Jesus, making us true partners with the Father and the Son. This is the inheritance of the new spiritual self, created in the image of God in righteousness and holiness. This is our rightful experience, our work, our joy, and our crown. Even though we may still sin, these sins are under the grace and atonement of Christ's blood. Our sins cannot diminish our fellowship with the Father and His Son, Jesus Christ, nor can they reduce our complete joy or bring back the fear of death to our consciences, which have been purified by the eternal Spirit of Christ's sacrifice.

The Source of Conflict Between Flesh and Spirit

As previously mentioned, the flesh—composed of mere flesh and bones—cannot be inherently deemed the source of sin or evil, for it is part of God's creation. God does not create evil. However, the nature of sin inherited from Adam represents a *"fallen freedom,"* disconnected from its divine origin, which once safeguarded and managed it. This fallen state is marked by an unrestrained will and corrupted desires, coupled with a degraded and separated knowledge from God. All these elements have become instruments in the devil's hands. Consequently, the flesh, as long as it is controlled by these corrupting forces, loses its purpose and value.

God, therefore, intended to create us a new — a spiritual rebirth from above — totally separated from the origins and consequences of sin. This rebirth reflects the nature of Christ's resurrected body, which has abolished sin and conquered death for the new creation. This is why the Apostle John's statement is both accurate and critical: *"No one born of God sins; he cannot sin"* (1 John.3:9). This new man, inherited from Christ as the second Adam, represents our new Father in place of Adam. This new creation grants us adoption with God the Father, and Christ is called our firstborn (Rom.8:29) and the firstborn from the dead (Col.1:18). Although we are considered created in Him and in His image, it is vital to recognize that our new spiritual body does not sin or die, being united with Christ Jesus: *"I no longer live, but Christ lives in me"* (Gal.2:20). *"But whoever is united with the Lord is one with him in spirit"* (1 Cor.6:17). *"You are in me, and I am in you"* (John.14:20). *"Whoever believes in me, though they die, will live; and everyone who lives and believes in me will never die"* (John.11:25-26). The conflict, therefore, is not within the nature of each body but within their will and understanding. The old body is governed by earthly desires — worldly pleasures that Adam, our forefather, succumbed to. Its understanding is confined to material realities and the limits of the intellect. Spiritual matters, which transcend human reason, are seen as ignorance by the old body. Some might claim that God is known through intellect alone, but this is deceptive. God is known only through faith, which comes from spiritual awareness.

Thus, the struggle is between the rational mind of the old body and the spiritual awareness of the new man, who is connected to God. These cannot meet or align except under the authority of submission and surrender to God. As a result, those with natural simplicity avoid engaging with profound divine knowledge that only spiritual awareness can grasp. Instead, they accept basic beliefs without questioning.

This truth is evident in the disciples, who could not understand the reality of Christ or recognize His person until Christ opened their minds (Luke.24:45) through a special spiritual insight provided by the Holy Spirit, setting the stage for the new spiritual body's manifestation on Pentecost. Thus, the struggle exists between the old body and the new spiritual man, between awareness of divine truth and the deception and falsification produced by the old body. The old body presents worldly glory, power, pleasures, desires, and all forms of deceit as essential and significant, while the new man, marked by righteousness and divine truth, judges all these as lies and trivialities, distancing himself and resisting them, even at a personal cost.

In the end, the person who succumbs to the old body faces regret and sorrow, awaiting judgment. In contrast, the person who overcomes through their spiritual self, reflecting righteousness and divine truth, experiences victory, complete joy, and anticipation of future glory: *"For those who are led by the Spirit of God are the children of God... If we are children, then we are heirs — heirs of God and co-heirs with Christ"* (Rom.8:14, 17).

The Nature of the New Man

So, what exactly is the nature of the new man? In essence, the new man is characterized by the nature of the risen Christ—spiritual, justified, and ready for a new life in fellowship with the Father and His Son, Jesus Christ. When invigorated by the gospel and prayer, this new nature becomes receptive to understanding the mysteries of the Word, grasping the truth, and discovering God's purposes and plans. It is graced to be a true temple of the Holy Spirit, who dwells within, guides, comforts, teaches, and reveals the truths of Christ as promised. Additionally, this nature is open to visions, revelations, and spiritual gifts, freely given without measure. Paul views this nature as fitting for being a part of Christ's body, and the Church adorns herself with such saints throughout history.

Paul affirms that this new nature, which is open to Christ's perfect love, is also deserving of being filled with all the fullness of God: "*And to know this love that surpasses knowledge—that you may be filled to the measure of all the fullness of God*" (Eph.3:19). This divine preparation means that believers are becoming one unified body in Christ, continuously transformed from one degree of glory to another, yet maintaining a singular essence. This collective growth aims for unity in faith and knowledge of the Son of God, reaching full maturity: "*To equip his people for works of service, so that the body of Christ may be built up until we all reach unity in the faith and in the knowledge of the Son of God and become mature, attaining to the whole measure of the fullness of Christ*" (Eph.4:12-13).

If our ultimate goal is to be united as one complete being with the fullness of Christ's stature, it is crucial to understand the significance of loving one another. This love is not merely a requirement but an essential characteristic. As Paul instructs: *"Instead, speaking the truth in love, we will grow to become in every respect the mature body of him who is the head, that is, Christ"* (Eph.4:15).

On the other hand, love expressed through the old nature is deceitful and false. True love alone comes from God, who is the very essence of love. The new spiritual nature, unlike the old one, embodies this true love. Genuine love does not stem from personal emotion, duty, or bravery. For instance, a person might die for a loved one out of affection, a servant might die for their faithfulness, or a soldier might die for their courage. However, a spiritual person loves out of love for God and for God's sake, willing to deny themselves and sacrifice, reflecting God's nature. This love is an extension of God's own love. In contrast, the old nature's love is driven by personal emotions or human ideals, lacking any heavenly reward. Spiritual love, rooted in the new man's nature, comes from God's love for others, without seeking personal gain or driven by instinctual urges.

The true measure of this spiritual love is demonstrated by the command to *"Love your enemies,"* in light of: *"But God demonstrates his own love for us in this: While we were still sinners, Christ died for us"* (Rom.5:8) and *"For if, while we were God's enemies, we were reconciled to him through the death of his Son"* (Rom.5:10) and *"The Son of God, who loved me and gave himself for me"* (Gal.2:20).

These examples of love reflect the nature of Christ that we inherit through faith and baptism in His name. So, what defines a true Christian? The answer is unmistakable: they love their enemies. The genuine love emerging from the depth of the new man's nature is described by Peter: *"Now that you have purified yourselves by obeying the truth so that you have sincere love for each other, love one another deeply, from the heart. For you have been born again, not of perishable seed, but of imperishable, through the living and enduring word of God"* (1 Peter.1:22-23). Peter's emphasis on "*sincere love*" highlights that it is free from the passions and inclinations of the old nature.

The New Man and the Kingdom

What is the connection between the new man and the Kingdom of God? The new spiritual identity we receive through faith in Christ and baptism is what makes us children of God, born of God. This new nature is the key to inheriting the Kingdom with Christ: "*The Spirit himself testifies with our spirit that we are God's children. Now if we are children, then we are heirs—heirs of God and co-heirs with Christ"* (Rom.8:16-17). This implies that our salvation will be fully realized when our new spiritual self is freed from the limitations of our physical body. Paul reflects this idea: "*For we know that if the earthly tent we live in is destroyed, we have a building from God, an eternal house in heaven, not built by human hands. Meanwhile we groan, longing to be clothed instead with our heavenly dwelling, because when we are clothed, we will not be found naked. For while we are in this tent, we groan and are burdened, because we do not wish to be unclothed but to be clothed instead with our heavenly dwelling, so that what is mortal may be swallowed up by life. Now the one who has fashioned us for this very purpose is God, who has given us the Spirit as a deposit, guaranteeing what is to come"* (2 Cor.5:1-5).

Paul compares our current earthly existence to living in a temporary tent, while our new spiritual existence is like an eternal heavenly home. This new man or spirit acts as a guarantee of our eternal life with God.

The New Body and Judgment

What about judgment? As previously mentioned, the new body is born of God. According to John, those born of God do not sin and cannot sin because they possess God's nature and Spirit. This makes them completely separate from the concept of sin and the law that only applies to the physical body. Moreover, they are entirely free from the penalty of death inherited from Adam. Thus, it is confidently stated that they cannot face judgment, as Paul writes: *"Therefore, there is now no condemnation for those who are in Christ Jesus"* (Rom.8:1). We are indeed in Christ Jesus through faith and baptism, based on the atonement and salvation. Even when considering the continuation of the verse, *"who do not live according to the flesh but according to the Spirit,"* it clarifies the meaning of *"those who are in Christ Jesus,"* rather than adding to it. Thus, a Christian who lives by faith and the gifts of the new man—engaging in a relationship with God, worship, prayer, and sincere love for others—will not face judgment. They are already considered to be in Christ Jesus, living in the fellowship of eternal life as a foretaste, with the hope of living with Him forever and inheriting the Kingdom as God's child in Christ.

John emphasizes this assurance when he writes: *"Dear friends, now we are children of God, and what we will be has not yet been made known. But we know that when Christ appears, we shall be like him, for we shall see him as he is"* (1 John.3:2). John confirms that we will stand in our new identity received through baptism by putting on Christ, when we shed our old self through physical death and meet Christ above.

When Christ is revealed, we will be like Him, reflecting what we have received here because we are created in the image of God in righteousness and holiness. John's statement, *"we shall be like Him,"* is rooted in the promise that *"we shall see Him as He is,"* meaning that when we see Him, He will be as He is in us. This provides a powerful and comforting vision of faith.

CHAPTER THREE

DIVINE DESIGN:
FROM CREATION TO REDEMPTION AND RESURRECTION

The Divine Plan: Understanding the First and Second Creation

When we explore the concepts of the first and second creations, we find that their stages are arranged and managed with divine precision in a manner that is both awe-inspiring and profound. Observing the divine revelation reveals how these stages interweave in a way that defies description but is remarkably clear to those who seek spiritual insight from God. This clarity mirrors the revelations given to the Apostle Paul, whose teachings guide us in understanding this profound divine plan.

The First Stage of Human Creation : "Before the Foundation of the World ".

1.*The Origin of Humanity* : According to the Apostle Paul's letter to the Ephesians, God's initial intention was to create humanity to stand before Him and praise His blessings. As stated in Ephesians 1:3: *"Blessed be the God and Father of our Lord Jesus Christ, who has blessed us with every spiritual blessing in the heavenly places in Christ."* This verse unveils the first aspect of human creation: humanity was intended to receive every spiritual blessing in the heavenly realms, blessed by God with an eternal blessing. The phrase *"every spiritual blessing in the heavenly places"* implies a complete and absolute divine act. Humanity is endowed with all heavenly gifts and blessings, with no reference to earthly or physical creation at this stage. The addition of *"in Christ"* indicates that these blessings are bestowed through Jesus Christ, implying that these divine privileges are granted in union with Christ, the Son of God.

2.*Election and Holiness*: The subsequent verse, Ephesians 1:4, states: *"He chose us in Him before the foundation of the world, that we should be holy and without blame before Him in love."* This verse clarifies the previous one by showing that God's blessing of spiritual gifts is based on His choice to *"choose us in Christ."* This means God's choice for humanity is based on being united with Christ, all within the scope of God's eternal plan. Before the world was created, Christ was *"the Word."* Thus, human creation was determined in the blessed Son to be united with Him, sharing in His blessings, being sanctified, and blameless in Him. The scriptures specify that this creation exists *"before God,"* in His presence. Revelation 7:15 highlights this: *"Therefore they are before the throne of God, and serve Him day and night in His temple."* The essential relationship of this heavenly creation with God is one of love, a love that extends from the relationship between the Son and the Father to this creation through its union with the Son.

3.*Adoption*: Ephesians 1:5 further explains: *"Having predestined us to adoption as sons by Jesus Christ to Himself, according to the good pleasure of His will."* This verse clarifies that God predestined us for adoption before the foundation of the world, establishing our personal relationship with Him as His children. Since no creation can attain the status of a child of God on its own, adoption through union with the Son was necessary to ensure a state of divine permanence, holiness, and love. Paul emphasizes that this adoption is *"to Himself,"* reflecting God's profound desire for children through adoption. The phrase *"according to the good pleasure of His will"* reveals a deep-seated joy in God's heart. God delighted in adopting humanity as His children through their union with His Son, reflecting a divine pleasure marked by paternal joy.

4.*Praise of His Glory:* Finally, Ephesians 1:6 reveals the ultimate purpose of humanity's creation, blessing, sanctification, union with the Son, and adoption: *"To the praise of the glory of His grace, which He has freely given us in the Beloved."* This indicates that humanity's primary function is to stand before God *"to the praise of the glory of His grace,"* akin to angels but in a higher degree, as children surpass servants. The divine revelation thus provides a clear picture of God's intention for humanity to be a blessed, sanctified, and united creation standing before Him in His presence, dedicated to praising and glorifying His grace. This divine grace, given through Christ, forms the foundation of humanity's creation before the world began, illustrating the profound joy of God's will and His love for His Son. Ultimately, humanity is envisioned as the closest and most beloved creation, united with the Son, tasked with praising and glorifying the grace of God.

The Second Stage of Human Creation:

In the second stage of creation, God did not start with the heavenly nature and its blessings or with the union with the Son. Instead, He began with man's creation from the earth, intending to elevate him through various stages, eventually leading him from the earth to the heavens. This progression reflects God's profound wisdom, patience, and mastery. Ultimately, His creation must testify to this journey from its very core and experiences. This process unfolds in two distinct stages: the first in paradise, and the second in the descent to the earth.

1.*The First Stage, In Paradise*: The creation of man from the earth is detailed in the Book of Genesis. God breathed life into man, transforming him into a living being. God's design was for man to be made in His own image and likeness — not merely in external appearance, but in the essence that would be fully revealed in time. Genesis describes God's creation of man as "*very good.*" However, we struggle to understand the full extent of this goodness and the significance of the term "*very*" as used by God. For God, this designation implies an extraordinary and profound value. When we look at ourselves, we often fail to see this inherent goodness or its intensification. Therefore, God's original creation was indeed a close reflection of Himself, thanks to His divine breath. This closeness is why God kept man in the Garden of Eden, a state of eternal life.

Adam's earthly nature was endowed with spiritual qualities and high attributes, enabling him to be in the presence of God, communicate with Him, and receive divine knowledge through an inner, intellectual dialogue rather than through spoken words or auditory senses. This method of communication reflects gifts that belong more to the spirit than to the physical body. Similarly, Adam's emotions and feelings were not purely physical but were perceived through the deeper spiritual essence of his soul. His conscience, developed through a close relationship with God and influenced by divine love, served as a profound internal center within him, representing a miniature reflection of divine justice and truth. This conscience was a vital inheritance from God, symbolizing the spiritual legacy of the lost paradise and a faint reminder of a close relationship with the divine.

[47]

The conscience and spiritual awareness, as legacies from paradise, are incredibly refined instruments for thought and spiritual insight. While the intellect operates within their framework, it cannot match their depth, precision, and timeless nature. When activated by spiritual pursuits, the conscience can grasp higher realities from beyond the physical world, whether these are religious, musical, or artistic. These manifestations represent the highest aspects of human spiritual awareness, showcasing one of humanity's greatest gifts from God. Such spiritual awareness, whether in religion, literature, music, or art, reveals humanity's origins and future direction. It can achieve extraordinary levels of understanding, similar to a child performing masterpieces by the greatest composers, a young poet crafting profound verses, or a saintly figure discussing divine mysteries and future visions. These are treasures from the human spiritual reservoir that have retained their brilliance over time, reflecting not just humanity's past but its potential future when it realizes its original divine intent.

Both the conscience and spiritual awareness, along with the intellectual communication with God, internal listening, and spiritual emotions, are fundamental aspects of human creation inherited from God's breath. They signify a divine likeness that transcends the earthly realm. When the physical body ceases with death, these spiritual treasures remain, integrating into the new spiritual creation. However, it was evident that an earthly creation could not sustain eternal alignment with God. After a period, the earthly nature proved incapable of maintaining its divine likeness. Adam and Eve, using the free will and knowledge bestowed upon them by God, transgressed His command, seeking to gain knowledge of good and evil. This act led them to lose their state of divine obedience and guidance, falling from their perfect nature into a realm of moral ambiguity.

This fall does not imply that God's creation of humanity was flawed or defective. Rather, God created man from the earth and endowed him with divine breath, intending that any elevation would come through divine will and power, not mere human effort. The intended progression was a transformation from human nature to divine likeness, facilitated by God's will. However, Adam's disobedience caused him to separate from God and fall from his balanced, perfect state, resulting in a loss of potential for further elevation and a subsequent decline. This demonstrated that the earthly creation could not sustain a divine life, necessitating its descent from the level that had once allowed it to reside in paradise with God, as it had lost the privilege of being with Him.

The punishment of death and the curse that befell Adam as a result of his disobedience was intrinsically tied to his earthly nature and was not an act of injustice from God. In essence, death represents a return to the earth. Therefore, the punishment of death was effectively a descent into the earth. The curse, meanwhile, signifies a fall from the divine presence, a separation from God's life-giving presence — an outcome directly resulting from Adam's own actions.

However, death, when viewed as a return to the earth, was actually an act of divine mercy. It prevented humanity from suffering eternally in its state of imperfection and limitation. Death, in this sense, carried a promise of hope: once humanity's limitations and shortcomings had been fully exhausted, God could elevate it to a state free from such deficiencies. The necessity of death and the curse arose from humanity's inherent imperfections. By accepting these conditions, humanity could eventually be restored by God to its original, perfected state, thereby overcoming death and the curse.

2. *The second stage, the descent into the earth*: unfolds in two distinct phases, illustrating how humanity's once-noble earthly nature became marred by imperfections and limitations.

1. *The first phase of human history* , which began with Adam and Eve and extended to their descendants, presents a fascinating and perplexing aspect of human history: the extraordinarily long lifespans of these early figures. Adam, for instance, lived for 930 years before his death. His son Seth lived for 912 years, and Seth's son Enosh lived for 905 years. Enosh's descendant Kenan lived for 910 years, while his son Mahalalel reached 895 years. Jared, another descendant, lived for 962 years, and Enoch lived for 365 years before being taken by God, avoiding death. Enoch's son Methuselah lived for 969 years, the longest lifespan recorded before his death. This pattern of immense longevity continued until Noah, who lived for 950 years.

The remarkable consistency of these long lifespans — hovering around 900 years — raises intriguing questions. What kind of humans were these, and what were their physical attributes? How could their brains and bodies sustain such functionality for nearly a millennium? What kind of cells, heart, muscles, and veins could maintain health and vitality for such an extended period without deteriorating?

This extraordinary longevity suggests that the early descendants of Adam retained significant traces of the original, perfect state in which God created humanity. When modern anthropologists hear of individuals living for nearly a thousand years, it challenges their understanding and existing scientific frameworks. Such lifespans seem to defy the limits of rational thought and medical science, hinting at a nature far beyond our current comprehension. These ancient beings, who lived under conditions that vastly differ from those of today, still bore the marks of their divine Creator before the wear of time and human errors began to take their toll.

2. *The second phase of human history*, began with Abraham, marking a dramatic and swift decline in lifespans. Abraham himself lived to be 175 years old before passing away. From this point on, human lifespans decreased rapidly. By the time of King David, the average lifespan had dropped to around 70 years, and in times of hardship, it was often as short as 80 years, reflecting the wear and tear of life's challenges (Ps.90:10).

This significant reduction in lifespan signified a deeper decline in human nature, influenced by the cumulative effects of aging, diseases, and ignorance. Time became a crucial factor in humanity's decline, with the earthly nature of humans reaching its most frail and limited state. As a result, the moral and behavioural standards of humanity deteriorated, reflecting a state of curse and distance from God.

In this weakened state, all natural attributes of humanity were eroded. God intervened to fulfil His eternal purpose by transforming humanity from its weakened earthly condition to a new, elevated state. Through Christ, humanity was granted a transition from its earthly nature to a heavenly one, blessed with eternal benefits. This transformation marked the beginning of the third Stage in human evolution.

The Third Stage of Human Creation:

The Preparation and Revelation of the Divine Plan: It has become clear that the transformation or renewal of human nature must come from an external source, specifically from God Himself, according to

His eternal purpose and plan established before the foundation of the world. This transformation involves not only an individual standing before God but being "*in Christ Jesus*" as part of the divine arrangement: "*He chose us in Him before the foundation of the world*" (Eph.1:4). From the outset, the fundamental and enduring connection in human creation has been with Christ, who empowers humanity to live before God in heaven and to praise Him, based on the "*grace*" provided through Christ Jesus. Thus, the foundation of human creation is God's grace in Christ.

Initiation of the Plan, "Before the Foundation of the World": For humanity to rise from its earthly nature to a state of heavenly existence, it was necessary to completely abandon the earthly nature burdened by mortality and the curse accumulated over centuries. This allowed for the reception of a new creation with a new human nature, rooted in Christ and derived from His essence. We understand that the plan for humanity's creation was conceived "before the foundation of the world," meaning before time began, in eternity. We also recognize that human creation was designed for eternal and everlasting existence in Christ in heaven: "*Blessed us with every spiritual blessing in the heavenly places in Christ, as He chose us in Him before the foundation of the world, that we should be holy and without blame before Him in love*" (Eph.1:3-4). Therefore, it is evident that God's plan began "*in Christ*" and "*before the foundation of the world,*" in eternity, where Christ was the "*Word,*" the self-revealing and acting nature of God. It was predetermined that the "*Word*" would be responsible for creating humanity and would create humanity from His own nature.

*Timing of the Plan, "When the Fullness of Time Had Come ":*The phrase "*when the fullness of time had come*" indicates that the period of human estrangement from God, characterized by suffering and the limitations of earthly existence, had reached its end. Humanity had fulfilled its punishment and curse on earth, and it was now time for God's favour and salvation to begin elevating humanity from the earth, ushering in a new creation according to His eternal plan. This means that as earthly movements were about to commence, corresponding actions in heaven regarding "*Christ*," the "*Word*," were also necessary. The initiation on earth required that heaven had completed its preparations to start the new creation simultaneously in both realms.

Preparation for the Revelation of the Plan: The preparation for the revelation of the plan occurred on two levels: what transpired in heaven in preparation for the new creation of humanity, and what took place on earth to prepare for this new creation. The Apostle Paul provides insight into what happened in heaven:

"*Let this mind be in you which was also in Christ Jesus — the Word in heaven — who, being in the form of God, did not consider it robbery to be equal with God. But made Himself of no reputation, taking the form of a servant, and coming in the likeness of men*" (Phil.2:5-7). "*But when the fullness of time had come, God sent forth His Son, born of a woman*" (Gal.4:4).

From this, we understand that for God to send His Son, the Word, who eternally exists in the form of God, He had to first empty Himself. This self-emptying involved relinquishing the divine glory (without abandoning His divine nature) to take on human form, enabling Him to appear as a man without causing fear, while still performing divine actions. This self-emptying of the Son marked the initial phase in the creation of the new humanity, a process that was completed in heaven.

On Earth, God orchestrated a series of profound historical events to prepare for the Son's arrival. While detailing every aspect is beyond the scope here, a brief summary captures the essence. God appointed a Roman emperor who expanded the empire's reach across the known world, unifying diverse regions under Roman authority. This consolidation spread the Greek and Roman languages across the empire, standardizing communication. Significant infrastructure improvements were made, including the construction of roads that facilitated safe and efficient travel for merchants to Rome. Roman judicial systems were established throughout the territories, ensuring stability and justice. All these measures collectively readied the world for the arrival of the heavenly King sent by God.

The Emergence of the Celestial Creation, "God Sent His Son, Born of a Woman": We have understood that the "*Word,*" the Son of God, humbled Himself by relinquishing the divine glory to come to Earth and assume human form. This was necessary to complete the creation of the new humanity. Indeed, the Word took on a human body, born of the Holy Spirit and the Virgin Mary, and was called by the angel before His birth: "*the Holy One, the Son of God.*" He appeared as a man and experienced every stage of human development. In essence, the Son, the Word, represented the ultimate, highest, and most sacred model of the new humanity from His birth to His ascension into heaven. Hence, He is referred to as the Second Adam or the New Adam, the father of the new creation.

Although His nature was truly human, as it was derived from a human mother, it was also divine, being the Son of God. This nature was both heavenly and sacred. Despite His human appearance, He was, in truth, the Word, the Son of God, existing in the divine image. Thus, God created a celestial prototype of the new humanity—an ideal, perfect, and sacred model that began to separate from the earthly realm and was prepared for a divine, heavenly life united with the holy Son.

However, the difference between the incarnate Word's nature and earthly human nature was immense—comparable to the difference between the dust of the earth and the holiness of heaven or between negative and positive forces. This disparity becomes clear when we recognize that the Son of God's nature is heavenly and sacred, whereas human nature had deteriorated to a state of frailty and corruption. Over thousands of years, human nature had accumulated experiences of impurity, depravity, lust, and various vices, alongside severe moral degradation including murder, lies, hatred, enmity, theft, and cruelty. Human nature was deeply tainted and dominated by these experiences.

Before humanity could adopt its new, sacred, and heavenly nature, it was necessary to purge both the human nature and the individual of its frailties and accumulated experiences from the earthly world. Human nature had to be emptied of its earthly deficiencies and impurities to receive a new, celestial nature capable of standing before God.

Therefore, the incarnate Son of God had to address two tasks simultaneously for humanity: He had to remove the earthly frailties and accumulated experiences from human nature and provide a new divine nature and essence from His own holy self, enabling humanity to achieve its heavenly perfection and stand before God. Indeed, the incarnate Word agreed with the Father's plan to take upon Himself all the defects, shame, and flaws of human nature, including the punishment of death and curse affecting human nature. Thus, according to the divine plan, the Son stood before God not merely as humanity's representative, but as one who bore humanity's punishment in His body and soul, receiving the judgment of death and curse on behalf of humanity.

But how did the incarnate Son of God take upon Himself human sins, death, and curse? From the beginning of Christ's ministry, God's plan was revealed through the offering of His Son, bearing human sin as a sacrifice on the cross. John the Baptist first announced this plan: "*Behold the Lamb of God who takes away the sin of the world*" (John.1:29), referring to Him as the sin offering for the world. Christ confirmed this plan by repeatedly stating that He would suffer, be crucified, die, and rise again on the third day.

This signified that according to the Father's plan, Christ agreed to be the atonement for human sins, bearing the punishment of death and curse on the cross, thus completing humanity's redemption. This plan was established before the foundation of the world, as Peter testified: "*Knowing that you were not redeemed with perishable things like silver or gold from your futile way of life inherited from your forefathers, but with precious blood, as of a lamb unblemished and spotless, the blood of Christ, known before the foundation of the world but has appeared in these last times for you*" (1 Peter.1:18-20).

The Nature of Christ's Redemption: Understanding the Atonement

The essence of Christ's monumental act of redemption is that He did not merely bear humanity's sins or accept the penalty of death as an external substitute. Instead, Christ's act of redemption occurred within humanity itself. As the incarnate Son of God, He took on human flesh and, being sinless, bore all of humanity's sins and transgressions in His holy body. Thus, Christ embodied the old, earthly human nature in its entirety and stood before God as if He were humanity itself, with all its sins. Simultaneously, He remained the Son who came to perfect humanity within Himself.

Examining the events in Gethsemane reveals a crucial phase in the hidden process of redemption between the Father and the Son. In Gethsemane, the Word, who had emptied Himself, began the first act of redemption by initiating the creation of a new, heavenly nature for humanity. The second act was the incarnation, where the Word, having emptied Himself of divine glory (though not of divinity), took on human form — forever linking humanity with God.

The pivotal question now is: How did Christ redeem humanity from death and the curse? In Gethsemane, we see Christ in deep distress, praying intensely to the Father *"with loud cries and tears"* (Heb.5:7) and, as described in the Gospels, praying *"with fervent intensity, and His sweat was like drops of blood falling to the ground"* (Luke.22:44). He confessed to His disciples that His soul was *"overwhelmed with sorrow to the point of death"* (Matt.26:38). The reason for Christ's anguish is revealed by His repeated plea for the Father to "take this cup" from Him.

What is this cup? Many theologians have debated this, with some suggesting it represented a fear of death, implying that Christ was ultimately terrified. This interpretation fails to align with Christ's character. Christ faced death with the same courage as martyrs who joyfully embraced it because of their hope. So, why would Christ, having emptied Himself and become incarnate, plead so desperately? His statement, *"It was for this very reason I came to this hour"* (John.12:27), reveals the profound purpose of

His suffering and death, indicating it was essential to complete His redemptive work.

In Gethsemane, Christ's reference to "*this cup*" symbolizes His acceptance of humanity's sins and disgrace, which He would bear publicly on the cross. This cup represented the weight of all human sin — adultery, murder, blasphemy — and the accompanying shame. Before taking on this immense burden, Christ faced the profound decision of whether He would accept embodying these sins and facing crucifixion. How could the Holy Son of God, who is sinless, accept such a fate? Death and condemnation are typically reserved for sinners, not the Holy One.

Christ's intense anguish in Gethsemane, where He prayed fervently three times to have the cup removed, was not merely fear of death. It was the deep suffering of accepting humanity's sins and the curse that comes with them. His struggle was not with the physical death itself but with the spiritual weight of becoming the embodiment of sin and disgrace while remaining united with the Father.

Despite His personal distress, Christ's submission to the Father's will was profound. He accepted the necessity of bearing humanity's sins due to His incarnation — taking on human nature and its burden. After three earnest pleas, Christ ultimately surrendered to the Father's will, saying, *"Not My will, but Yours be done"* (Luke.22:42). This act of surrender was the pinnacle of His redemptive mission.

Gethsemane is therefore central to the redemption narrative. Here, Christ faced the reality of taking on humanity's sins and enduring the curse. His trials before the Jewish council, Herod, and Pontius Pilate were part of a formal, global condemnation process. Christ's silence in these trials — whether before the Sanhedrin, Herod, or Pilate — highlighted His acceptance of judgment and condemnation on behalf of humanity. This silence emphasized the gravity of His sacrifice: bearing the weight of sin while maintaining His divine purity and holiness.

In His ultimate act of redemption, Christ chose not to defend Himself or counter the accusations laid against Him during His trials. His silence before the judges, which astonished Pontius Pilate, was a profound acceptance of the charges brought against Him. Pilate, as a judge, recognized that Christ's refusal to speak or defend Himself implied the truth of the accusations, meaning that Christ willingly accepted the guilt for the sins attributed to Him. Thus, the judgment passed upon Him was deemed just, as He had accepted the weight of these sins.

Christ bore all human sins, including accusations of blasphemy, corruption, and wrongdoing. The gravest of these was blasphemy, which warranted crucifixion. By choosing to be crucified, Christ affirmed what St. Peter stated: *"He Himself bore our sins in His body on the tree"* (1 Peter.2:24). He was crucified and died as a result. Furthermore, *"Christ redeemed us from the curse of the law, having become a curse for us, for it is written: 'Cursed is everyone who is hanged on a tree'"* (Gal.3:13).

In this act of redemption, Christ's sacrifice takes on its fullest significance. He died on the cross carrying the sins and curses of humanity, was buried, and remained in the grave for three days to fully experience death. His body bore the entirety of human sin, curse, and shame. It is crucial to understand that the sins and curse Christ bore were not His own; He remained sinless and holy. His resurrection was therefore essential: He rose with the very human body that had died, having fully endured the penalty of death and the curse. This resurrection transformed His human body into a new, pure, and holy form, victorious over sin, death, and the grave. As Christ ascended to heaven with the body in which

He had died and risen, He demonstrated the divine power that will ultimately elevate us from death and earth, assuring us that we too will be raised to dwell with Him in heaven.

The Revelation and Fulfilment: The New Resurrected Body

Christ has delivered the new resurrected body, which triumphed over death and the abyss, to all who believe in Him. This act represents the culmination of the grand redemptive work accomplished by the Word, the Son of God incarnate. By ascending with the body He took from humanity, Christ did so as the new humanity, embodying the ultimate model of the new creation. This new humanity, created by Christ from His own being and according to His own image, maintains a complete relationship with the Father: *"Righteous Father, though the world does not know You, I know You; and they know that You have sent Me. I have made You known to them, and will continue to make You known in order that the love You have for Me may be in them and that I myself may be in them"* (John.17:25-26). Thus, Christ has prepared the new humanity for ascension and eternal life with God in heaven.

The next phase was to impart a complete sample of this resurrected body of Christ, glorified by God, to every believer through baptism. This sacrament represents the *"mystery of the new creation,"* which is invisible to human perception, or the *"mystery of the second birth from above by the Spirit of Christ"* for all who confess, believe, and bear witness to the death and resurrection of Christ on the cross. But what does this mean?

It means that through His incarnation, death, and resurrection, Christ created within Himself the new man—complete, holy, and pure—who possesses divine son-ship in the Word, the only Son, both before and after the incarnation. The Son of God took on human form with all that was His, yet He emptied Himself of divine glory to be seen as a man. On the cross, He completed the redemption of humanity and prepared it through the divine mystery to receive a new spiritual body from the resurrected Christ, replacing the old, earthly body that He had crucified. In baptism, the Father, the Son, and the Holy Spirit work together to remove the old, earthly body from humanity and clothe them with the new creation: *"You have put off the old man with his deeds (in baptism), and have put on the new man who is renewed in knowledge according to the image of Him who created him"* (Col.3:9-10).

If one finds it difficult to grasp this redemptive act as a genuine new creation, they should recall Christ's teaching to Nicodemus about the new birth from above through water and the Spirit. Christ explained: *"That which is born of the flesh is flesh, and that which is born of the Spirit is spirit. Do not marvel that I said to you, 'You must be born again.' The wind blows where it wishes, and you hear the sound of it, but cannot tell where it comes from and where it goes. So is everyone who is born of the Spirit"* (John.3:6-8). The new creation of humanity, the spiritual rebirth through water and the Spirit in baptism, is a supernatural act that is not visible because it occurs through the creative power of God in the divine mystery, much like all works of the Spirit. As the Apostle Paul explains, what happens in baptism mirrors what happened on the cross; just as Christ's death resulted in the death of the old man, so His resurrection brings forth the new man with a new nature secretly derived from Christ's resurrection.

This transformation changes the earthly "I" previously bound to the old body into the likeness of Christ's resurrected self: *"But we all, with unveiled face, beholding as in a mirror the glory of the Lord, are being transformed into the same image from glory to glory, just as by the Spirit of the Lord"* (2Cor.3:18); *"And put on the new man which was created according to God, in true righteousness and holiness"* (Ephesians 4:24); *"Who will transform our lowly body that it may be conformed to His glorious body"* (Phil.3:21).

It is important to understand that this new creation of humanity is not autonomous or independent. It is *"created in Christ"* and united with Him, never to be separated. This union with Christ is the essence of the new creation, ensuring its salvation, permanence, and its visibility in heaven, where it will forever praise God as a heavenly creation: *"For we are His workmanship, created in Christ Jesus for good works, which God prepared beforehand that we should walk in them"* (Eph.2:10). Thus, we have arrived at the final stage of redemption, achieving the new creation of humanity as God intended before the foundation of the world: *"Just as He chose us in Him before the foundation of the world, that we should be holy and without blame before Him in love, having predestined us to adoption as sons by Jesus Christ to Himself, according to the good pleasure of His will"* (Eph.1:4-5). The spiritual blessing with which God has blessed us in the heavenly realms is partially experienced now, and we eagerly await its fullness when we finally cast off the old body, anticipating the resurrection when the new man will be revealed in the brilliance of Christ's light.

The eternal and permanent existence of the new creation in the heavens with Christ, according to God's eternal plan, is explicitly stated: *"And raised us up together, and made us sit together in the heavenly places in Christ Jesus, that in the ages to come He might show the exceeding riches of His grace in His kindness toward us in Christ Jesus"* (Eph.2:6). The Apostle John adds, *"Beloved, now we are children of God, and it has not yet been revealed what we shall be. But we know that when He is revealed, we shall be like Him, for we shall see Him as He is. And everyone who has this hope in Him purifies himself, just as He is pure"* (1 John.3:2-3).

Let us earnestly appreciate how the creation of humanity has been God's focus from eternity past and remains so. Let us reflect on the depth of His condescension, His sacrifices, and His commitment to ultimately create humanity as a blessed heavenly creation endowed with every spiritual blessing in the heavenly realms. We should marvel at the precision and intentionality of each step in creation and the ensuing thousands of years, leading us to our ultimate purpose preserved in the heavens before the foundation of the world. This is so that we may live with God in a state of holiness and love, worthy of a spiritual creation that stands before God, forever praising Him and glorifying His grace.

CHAPTER FOUR

ETERNAL TRANSFORMATION: EMBRACING THE NEW CREATION AND ITS GOOD WORKS.

The Resurrection of Christ: The Revelation of the New Creation

In the second chapter of Paul's letter to the Ephesians, we find a clear definition of the new creation: *"For we are His workmanship, created in Christ Jesus for good works, which God prepared beforehand that we should walk in them"* (Eph.2:10). This passage reveals that good works are not merely a means to attain the new creation but are central to it. The new creation, bestowed upon us through the resurrection, is a pure gift of grace — unearned and freely given while we were still entrenched in sin. Despite this, once we receive this new creation and enter its vibrant realm, we are immediately called to engage in works fitting for it: *"And you He made alive, who were dead in trespasses and sins, in which you once walked according to the course of this world, according to the prince of the power of the air, the spirit who now works in the sons of disobedience, among whom also we all once conducted ourselves in the lusts of our flesh, fulfilling the desires of the flesh and of the mind, and were by nature children of wrath, just as the others. But God, who is rich in mercy, because of His great love with which He loved us, even when we were dead in trespasses, made us alive together with Christ (by grace you have been saved), and raised us up together, and made us sit together in the heavenly places in Christ Jesus, that in the ages to come He might show the exceeding riches of His grace in His kindness toward us in Christ Jesus. For by grace you have been saved through faith, and that not of yourselves; it is the gift of God, not of works, lest anyone should boast. For we are His workmanship, created in Christ Jesus for good works, which God prepared beforehand that we should walk in them"* (Eph.2:1-10).

From this passage, it's evident that the good works we are called to follow a divine plan prepared by God and revealed in the Gospel. They are not based on individual preferences but on a specific divine order that the Church, guided by the Spirit, can provide according to the measure of each person's grace. These good works aim to highlight the new man's position in the new life or the Spirit of resurrection he has received. All such works serve to witness to this new life in the present age, acting as a beacon to those in darkness and glorifying God, the Creator and Giver of this new creation.

Though the new creation operates within the present age, it fundamentally transcends it. Its purpose is to serve as a continuous testimony to the death and resurrection of Christ, reflecting a reality beyond the current age's understanding. Therefore, it is crucial to continually proclaim the truth of God's promises, fulfilled in time, supported by the Spirit's evidence and power. The new man is essentially created for this witness, and this witness by the Spirit is a good work in itself: *"created... for good works"* (Eph.2:10). If the new man ceases to witness to the Kingdom of God and the life of the age to come through his actions and behaviour, he effectively undermines his spiritual existence or buries his talent, disregarding his eternal inheritance. This is the very reason for which he was created — to testify daily to his eternal legacy, as *"if we are children, then we are heirs — heirs of God and joint heirs with Christ"* (Rom.8:17).

The Essential Path of Good Works for the New Creation: Reflecting Christ's Own Mission

The framework for good works, which ultimately seeks to glorify God and is required of the new creation who has risen from the dead, aligns seamlessly with Christ's own mission. Christ's resurrection was both to the glory of the Father and a means of glorifying the Father Himself: *"Just as Christ was raised from the dead by the glory of the Father, we too should walk in newness of life"* (Rom.6:4). Our new life, as those resurrected from the dead, is a testimony to the Father's glory: *"I have glorified You on the earth"* (John.17:4), and *"I have manifested Your name to the men"* (John.17:6).

To better understand this imperative for those living in the newness of life, Saint Paul underscores that Christ now lives to God, and thus, our lives should also be lived for God: *"For the death that He died, He died to sin once for all; but the life that He lives, He lives to God. Likewise you also, reckon yourselves to be dead indeed to sin, but alive to God in Christ Jesus our Lord"* (Rom.6:10-11). The essence of the new life is to bear witness to the glory of the Father.

Therefore, the purpose of good works for the new creation is defined by Christ's own mystery. Whether in action, thought, will, or intention, everything should be done *"for the glory of God"* (1 Cor.10:31). Just as Christ, after His resurrection, was *"for the glory of God the Father,"* so too is every individual in Christ, as a new creation, meant entirely for the glory of God the Father. This defined purpose of the new creation—empowered by Christ's resurrection and the outpouring of the Spirit of resurrection, which is the Spirit of holiness and renewal—addresses the failure of the old creation. The old creation was completely incapable of performing good works to glorify God, resulting instead in blasphemy and dishonour of God's great name.

Now, the role of the new creation is critical and significant compared to what the old creation failed to achieve, causing scandal to humanity and dishonouring God by distorting His image given to us at creation. The responsibility of the new man, born from above and bearing the nature of the new creation, is immense. It involves restoring a righteous relationship with God and renewing the dignity of His image to its fullest extent in relation to oneself, to God, and to others.

Firstly, in relation to oneself: The new creation responds to the evils that marred the divine image within—polluting the mind, will, conscience, and body. Good works serve to restore the true image of God in the new man, who is *"created according to God... in the image of his Creator"* (Eph.4:24; Col.3:10). *"You are slaves to the one whom you obey, whether of sin leading to death, or of obedience leading to righteousness. But thanks be to God that though you were slaves of sin, yet you obeyed from the heart that form of doctrine to which you were delivered. And having been set free from sin, you became slaves of righteousness. I speak in human terms because of the weakness of your flesh. For just as you presented your members as slaves to uncleanness, and of lawlessness leading to more lawlessness, so now present your members as slaves to righteousness for holiness"* (Rom.6:16-19).

Secondly, in relation to God: Good works glorify God, whereas previous disobedience and ignorance in the old nature led to blasphemy against the name of the Holy One: *"Let your light so shine before men, that they may see your good works and glorify your Father in heaven"* (Matt.5:16). Good works are deeply intertwined with prayer, spiritual service, and public praise to glorify God, positioning the new man among the heavenly hosts tasked with serving the Most High and honouring His holy name. This is a key goal of the new creation.

Thirdly, in relation to others: Ultimately, the good works of the new creation are directed towards others. They act as a proclamation of the New Covenant, a message of resurrection, and a demonstration of its transformative and joyous effect on human nature. This transformation moves from the dominion of darkness to the Kingdom of the Son of God. The testimony of those who bear witness to the resurrection is: *"I proclaim the praises of Him who called me out of darkness into His wonderful light"* (1 Peter.2:9). The new man's works are not for self-gratification but for the benefit of others, reflecting Jesus Christ's example who always sought to please the Father rather than Himself. This testimony is so compelling that anyone who experiences the joy of resurrection, tastes the goodness of the Lord, and perceives Christ's love cannot remain silent — it becomes like a fire in their bones.

For the old self, good works are a challenging and almost unattainable goal. Despite one's best efforts, these works often amount to a relentless battle against sin and its evil desires, or they are merely superficial actions that affect only the body or soul: *"Sanctify for the purification of the flesh!"* (Heb.9:13).

In contrast, for the new creation, good works are more than just a struggle against sin; they involve actively pursuing righteousness and holiness. From an evangelical standpoint, this is not merely about *"putting off the old man who is corrupt according to deceitful desires, with his deeds"* (Eph.4:22; Col.3:9), which addresses past wrongs and ignorance. Rather, good works for the new creation go beyond just removing the old self. They involve putting on the new self: *"And have put on the new man who is renewed in knowledge according to the image of Him who created him"* (Col.3:10).

The Nature of Good Works for the New Creation in Christ

Good works for the old creation are challenging, arduous, and nearly impossible. No matter how hard a person strives, their good deeds often amount to nothing more than a fierce battle against sin and its evil impulses, or mere superficial actions limited to the physical body or soul: *"to sanctify for the purification of the flesh"* (Heb.9:13). However, for the new creation, good works transcend the negative aspect of battling sin to include serving righteousness and holiness. In biblical terms, it is not merely about *"putting off the old man which grows corrupt according to the deceitful lusts"* (Eph.4:22; Col.3:9), which is simply paying off the massive debts incurred due to ignorance and self-deception. Rather, good works involve *"putting on the new man who is renewed in knowledge according to the image of Him who created him"* (Col.3:10).

Knowledge, in this context, is crucial. It is not merely a separate entity to be analysed in isolation from resurrection; there is no true knowledge without corresponding action, not even among angels. Spiritual knowledge, according to the new creation or New Covenant, is a divine gift rather than something earned through personal experience. This reflects the nature of divine truth: it is a gift bestowed upon the new creation. The new creation is described as having *"put on the new man who is renewed in knowledge according to the image of Him who created him"* (Col.3:10), where *"knowledge"* implies the fullness of true understanding. This means that the new creation increasingly resembles its Creator, renewed daily through a new understanding of Christ, the perfect model of God's image revealed to us.

The old creation was initially made in God's image, but sin distorted that image, leaving man devoid of righteousness, holiness, or truth. In contrast, God has now spiritually recreated man based on righteousness, holiness, and truth in the person of Jesus Christ, who is the first fruits of the new creation and the head of the new man. He embodies the essential image of God in humanity with glory and wonder through the mystery of ineffable perfection.

Thus, knowledge of Christ becomes the spiritual nourishment that helps us grow until Christ is formed in us, who is the image of God. Peter, however, reminds us that knowledge only benefits the new creation if it is free from deceit. Here, deceit refers to old, corrupted knowledge. The emphasis is on the purity of new knowledge, devoid of the flaws of old human thinking, which was based on personal skill and effort or misleading sin or falsely named knowledge. True knowledge aligns with Christ and the Spirit of resurrection and must be derived from the Holy Spirit and the Gospel: *"He will take what is Mine and declare it to you"* (John.16:14) and *"Lay aside all malice, all deceit, hypocrisy, envy, and all evil speaking... As new born babes, desire the pure milk of the word, that you may grow thereby, if indeed you have tasted that the Lord is gracious"* (1 Peter.2:1-3).

The phrase *"as new born babes"* highlights that knowledge is not about personal skill or effort but about longing, desire, and craving, much like a baby's craving for its mother's milk. Peter aligns with Paul in stating that the new creation grows and is renewed through true and complete knowledge of Christ, which is pure, untainted food—free from self-deception and sin. Genuine new knowledge of Christ, drawn from the Word, serves as nourishment for the new man and continually renews the image of God in him. Here, knowledge of Christ becomes spiritual sustenance for the new man's heart, conscience, and mind, growing daily, moving, thinking, and acting. This increases the desire for good works: *"Desire the pure milk of the word"* in proportion to tasting the goodness of Christ: *"If indeed you have tasted that the Lord is gracious."* Spiritual knowledge thus becomes a vital experience of truth, akin to food and drink for the spirit.

Renewal and transformation from glory to glory are key characteristics of genuine spiritual knowledge. False knowledge cancels out other knowledge, while the attribute of continuous renewal: *"And have put on the new man who is renewed in knowledge"* (Col.3:10) is essential due to constant interaction with the old self and deceitful knowledge. This interaction can weaken, harm, or obscure the light of spiritual understanding through sin or falsely named knowledge that falsely claims to challenge the Spirit's insights. Acceptance of continual change results from the enduring and infinite nature of divine truth and the boundless perfection of Christ, *"in whom are hidden all the treasures of wisdom and knowledge"* (Col.2:3).

Christ's love surpasses all understanding for humanity, and this will remain true even after the full transition to the afterlife. Thus, transformation from glory to glory is a fundamental aspect of spiritual vision, reflecting a profound aspiration towards the glory of Christ: *"But we all, with unveiled face, beholding as in a mirror the glory of the Lord, are being transformed into the same image from glory to glory, just as by the Spirit of the Lord"* (2 Cor.3:18).

True knowledge naturally leads to righteous and positive actions: *"As you have received Christ Jesus the Lord, so walk in Him, rooted and built up in Him and established in the faith, as you have been taught, abounding in it with thanksgiving"* (Col.2:6-7). When we fully embrace Christ and our understanding of Him is illuminated through the Gospel, this knowledge fosters a strong faith equivalent to genuine understanding. This knowledge is essentially a personal connection with the Holy Spirit, resulting from fellowship. Consequently, good works emerge from faith as a power flowing from an inexhaustible inner source and a warmth renewed daily through knowledge, that is, the Word. Therefore, once we fulfil the obligations of true knowledge—maintaining a personal relationship with Christ through love and prayer—we are equipped to perform good works driven by this fellowship and spiritual connection derived from Christ through the Gospel.

Good works can be divided into two main categories, which ultimately integrate to form a unified whole:

1. The First Category, Good Works as Efforts to Foster Unity Among Believers: Before delving into this aspect of good works, it's crucial to recognize that these actions—intended to achieve unity and togetherness, as Paul describes—are based on traits, qualities, and gifts granted by God to the new creation and embedded within its nature. The required good works and their execution were prepared by God in advance, establishing paths within our new nature. Thus, these works are firstly, a requirement; secondly, not considered meritorious upon completion, as all inspiration, strength, and motivation come from the Holy Spirit, making them integral to our creation; and thirdly, it is essential to fulfil these obligations before being eligible to engage in the second category of good works, which are granted by grace through the mysteries.

This illustrates the deep connection between knowledge and action for the new creation prepared for a spiritual life with Christ. Every gift and spiritual talent given by Christ through the Holy Spirit in our new life or new self is precisely measured to align perfectly with the possibility and necessity of our unity with others for the ultimate unity required for all redeemed and saved people. The foundation of all spiritual gifts from Christ is to enable us to achieve complete unity first with others and then with Christ as one body in the truest sense.

Thus, the positive nature of good works for the new creation is clearly defined. Such work cannot be considered good in the context of the new creation or resurrection unless it is aimed at and results in unity: unity that brings us together, and then unity with Christ. Paul's exhortation to the Ephesians is significant in this context: "*I, therefore, the prisoner of the Lord, beseech you to walk worthy of the calling with which you were called, with all lowliness and gentleness, with long-suffering, bearing with one another in love, endeavouring to keep the unity of the Spirit in the bond of peace. There is one body and one Spirit, just as you were called in one hope of your calling; one Lord, one faith, one baptism; one God and Father of all, who is above all, and through all, and in you all. But to each one of us grace was given according to the measure of Christ's gift*" (Eph.4:1-7). This captures the essence of the New Covenant and the new calling for every person in Christ, guiding good works towards a unified and happy end.

2. *The Second Category, Good Works as Free Grace Granted by God:* Life within the Church, when the congregation unites in prayer, worship, and

thanksgiving, reveals a preview of the future state of unity experienced in the present. The Church's unity in collective prayer is essentially a fellowship of gifts in the Spirit, practicing good works according to the measure of grace given to each individual in Christ and for the entire Church. Each person contributes to building up the body according to the gift bestowed by God. Public worship, therefore, confidently fosters the Church's growth for the Kingdom based on the diverse gifts that work for the unity of each person in the body of Christ.

As Paul states: "*He Himself gave some to be apostles, some prophets, some evangelists, and some pastors and teachers, for the equipping of the saints for the work of ministry, for the edifying of the body of Christ, till we all come to the unity of the faith and of the knowledge of the Son of God, to a perfect man, to the measure of the stature of the fullness of Christ... from whom the whole body, joined and knit together by what every joint supplies, according to the effective working by which every part does its share, causes growth of the body for the edifying of itself in love*" (Eph.4:11-16). Worship here is a fellowship of gifts working for the mystery of salvation, where the operation of gifts represents the pinnacle of all good works.

The Foundation of Good Works in the New Creation

It is crucial never to forget that talent is the foundation of good works for the new creation. As Paul the Apostle states, "*to create in Himself one new man from the two, thus making peace*" (Eph.2:15). This perspective transforms our understanding of worship, prayer, and praise into expressions of good works. These activities are not just rituals but are collective acts performed under Christ's inspiration, in one Spirit, to glorify God and promote unity. Therefore, all acts of worship are integral to the new creation and serve to establish and maintain the unity of believers in one body with Christ as the head, starting from now: *"Be filled with the Spirit, speaking to one another in psalms and hymns and spiritual songs, singing and making melody in your heart to the Lord, giving thanks always for all things to God the Father in the name of our Lord Jesus Christ, submitting to one another in the fear of God"* (Eph.5:18-21).

These acts of worship are deeply rooted in the Holy Spirit's guidance and are a direct result of being filled with Him. God has already prepared these good works for us to walk in. To elaborate on *"walking in them"*: this phrase implies that one should align their life and behaviour according to these principles, leading themselves by them and setting their conduct in accordance with their standards. Essentially, God has arranged spiritual works that match His goodness and our new nature, which we receive from Christ through the Holy Spirit. These works are in harmony with the spiritual gifts He pours out upon us, ensuring that these acts of *"worship"* become a defined and harmonious way of life, gladly submitting to God's will and plan rather than following our own desires. Consequently, there must be a process of self-discipline and submission of the flesh to allow the spiritual nature to prevail and for good worship to dominate, as will be discussed in the negative aspect of good works concerning sin and the flesh.

In the end, the fruits of the good works we offer to God are, in essence, profitable trades—the rewards derived from utilizing the talents given to us through our new nature, which we receive by Christ's resurrection. God, in accepting these profits from our talents, returns them to us in the form of abundant grace, blessings, and love: "*For if by the one man's offense death reigned through the one, much more those who receive abundance of grace and of the gift of righteousness will reign in life through the one, Jesus Christ*" (Rom.5:17). This additional overflow of grace propels the new creation toward greater acts of service, witness, and dedication, thus spreading throughout the world like leaven, as God's gifts continue to pour upon the new creation.

Types of Good Works for the New Creation in Christ Jesus

The good works required of us as a new creation in Christ Jesus, based on the gifts Christ has bestowed upon us, are categorized into two main types. As Paul the Apostle states, "*There are different kinds of gifts, but the same Spirit... distributing to each one individually as He wills*" (1 Cor.12:4, 11). These two types of works ultimately converge to achieve a unified goal: the unity of believers.

First Type, Negative Works: The first category encompasses the negative works that we must undertake as a new creation to counteract our former behaviours. These are efforts directed against the traits and habits of the old self, which were previously controlled by sin, passions, and deceptive desires.

Priority of Negative Struggle :Although this negative struggle aligns with the positive struggle of manifesting the traits of the new self, it is essential that the negative struggle comes first. Paul clarifies this with: "*And do this, knowing the time, that now it is high time to awake out of sleep; for now our salvation is nearer than when we first believed. The night is far spent, the day is at hand. Therefore let us cast off the works of darkness, and let us put on the armour of light*" (Rom.13:11-12). The process involves first shedding the old self and then adopting the new self.

"*You were taught, with regard to your former way of life, to put off your old self, which is being corrupted by its deceitful desires; to be made new in the attitude of your minds; and to put on the new self, created to be like God in true righteousness and holiness*" (Eph.4:22-24). "*Do not lie to each other, since you have taken off your old self with its practices and have put on the new self, which is being renewed in knowledge in the image of its Creator*" (Col.3:9-10).

But, What are the actions of the old self, and how do we fall into them? How do we rise to our new creation from them? The New Testament identifies the actions of the old self as follows:

- "*But what comes out of the mouth comes from the heart, and these defile a person. For out of the heart come evil thoughts—murder, adultery, sexual immorality, theft, false testimony, slander*" (Matt.15:18-19).

- "*But among you there must not be even a hint of sexual immorality, or of any kind of impurity, or of greed, because these are improper for God's holy people. Nor should there be obscenity, foolish talk, or coarse joking, which are out of place, but rather thanksgiving. For of this you can be sure: No immoral, impure, or greedy person—such a person is an idolater—has any inheritance in the kingdom of Christ and of God*" (Eph.5:3-5).

- "*But among you there must not be even a hint of sexual immorality, or of any kind of impurity, or of greed, because these are improper for God's holy people*" (Eph.5:12).

- *"Put to death, therefore, whatever belongs to your earthly nature: sexual immorality, impurity, lust, evil desires, and greed, which is idolatry. Because of these, the wrath of God is coming. You used to walk in these ways, in the life you once lived. But now you must also rid yourselves of all such things as these: anger, rage, malice, slander, and filthy language from your lips. Do not lie to each other"* (Col.3:5-9).

- *"Let us behave decently, as in the daytime, not in carousing and drunkenness, not in sexual immorality and debauchery, not in dissension and jealousy. Rather, clothe yourselves with the Lord Jesus Christ, and do not think about how to gratify the desires of the flesh"* (Rom.13:13-14).

- *"The acts of the flesh are obvious: sexual immorality, impurity, and debauchery; idolatry and witchcraft; hatred, discord, jealousy, fits of rage, selfish ambition, dissensions, factions and envy; drunkenness, orgies, and the like. I warn you, as I did before, that those who live like this will not inherit the kingdom of God"* (Gal.5:19-21).

- *"The one who sows to please his sinful nature, from that nature will reap destruction"* (Gal.6:8).

- *"If you live according to the flesh, you will die"* (Rom.8:13).

- *"Just as you used to offer the parts of your body in slavery to impurity and to ever-increasing wickedness, so now offer them in slavery to righteousness leading to holiness... What benefit did you reap at that time from the things you are now ashamed of? Those things result in death... For the wages of sin is death"* (Rom.6:19-23).

- *"Get rid of all bitterness, rage and anger, brawling and slander, along with every form of malice"* (Eph.4:31).

- *"The Spirit He caused to live in us envies intensely? But He gives us more grace"* (Jas.4:5-6).

- *"What causes fights and quarrels among you? Don't they come from your desires that battle within you? You desire but do not have, so you kill. You covet but cannot get what you want, so you quarrel and fight. You do not have because you do not ask God. When you ask, you do not receive, because you ask with wrong motives, that you may spend what you get on your pleasures... Don't slander one another"* (Jas. 4:1-12).

- *"They have become filled with every kind of wickedness, evil, greed, and depravity. They are full of envy, murder, strife, deceit, and malice. They are gossips, they are slanderers, God-haters, insolent, arrogant and boastful; they invent ways of doing evil; they disobey their parents; they have no understanding, no fidelity, no love, no mercy"* (Rom.1:29-31).

So, We can observe that the actions of the old self fall into two main categories:

1. *Actions Against God:* These include various forms of immorality, impurity, blasphemy, and idolatry. Immorality and impurity involve submitting the body and soul to unclean spirits rather than the Holy Spirit, leading to worship of impurity instead of holiness. The body should be united with the Spirit of God, not with unclean spirits: "*The body, however, is not meant for sexual immorality but for the Lord, and the Lord for the body*" (1 Cor.6:13). Idolatry, including the love of money and self-worship, represents dedicating the mind and conscience to worldly forces rather than God: "*Once you were alienated from God and were enemies in your minds because of your evil behaviour. But now he has reconciled you by Christ's physical body through death to present you holy in his sight, without blemish and free from accusation*" (Col.1:21-22)

2. *Actions Directed Against Others:* These actions are violations of others' rights, dignity, reputation, and well-being, leading to the fragmentation of unity and relationships between individuals at all levels. Thus, the evil actions of the old self, whether aimed at God or others, ultimately serve one malevolent purpose: to disrupt the unity between humans and God, and between humans themselves.

Therefore, How We Fall into the Evil Actions of the Old Self ,The reasons for falling into these actions can be summarized as follows:

1. *Knowledge of God Without Reverence:*

   - *"Although they knew God, they neither glorified Him as God nor gave thanks to Him, but their thinking became futile and their foolish hearts were darkened. Therefore, God gave them over in the sinful desires of their hearts to sexual impurity, for the degrading of their bodies with one another"* (Rom.1:21-24). This illustrates that having knowledge of God without honouring or worshiping Him leads to futile thinking and a darkened heart. This spiritual neglect results in falling into impurity and dishonouring of the body.

2. *Rejecting God's Presence in Our Lives:*

- *"They exchanged the truth of God for a lie, and worshiped and served created things rather than the Creator"* (Rom.1:25). When people refuse to keep God in their knowledge, they are given over to a depraved mind, resulting in a lack of moral clarity and righteous behaviour.

3. *Ignoring Divine Judgment:*

- *"Although they know God's righteous decree that those who do such things deserve death, they not only continue to do these very things but also approve of those who practice them"* (Rom.1:32). Knowing God's judgment yet ignoring it and taking pleasure in wrongdoing leads to a hardened heart and divine judgment.

4. *Worldly Conformity:*

- *"The god of this age has blinded the minds of unbelievers, so that they cannot see the light of the gospel that displays the glory of Christ, who is the image of God"* (2 Cor.4:4).Conforming to worldly values blinds individuals to the gospel, rendering the message of salvation ineffective and obscuring the truth.

5. *Avoidance of Spiritual Life:*

- *"As for you, you were dead in your transgressions and sins, in which you used to live when you followed the ways of this world and of the ruler of the kingdom of the air, the spirit who is now at work in those who are disobedient"* (Eph.2:1-2). Avoiding preaching and worship leads to spiritual ignorance, resulting in a loss of spiritual sensitivity and understanding.

6. *Childish Spirituality:*

    - *"Then we will no longer be infants, tossed back and forth by the waves, and blown here and there by every wind of teaching and by the cunning and craftiness of people in their deceitful scheming"* (Eph.4:14). Immature spiritual understanding and susceptibility to every new teaching lead to confusion and vulnerability to deception.

7. *Harbouring Anger and Sinful Influence:*

    - *"Do not give the devil a foothold. In your anger do not sin: Do not let the sun go down while you are still angry"* (Eph.4:27-26). Allowing anger and giving the devil a foothold can lead to increased sin and a pattern of wrongdoing.

8. *Alignment with Worldly Spirit:*

- *"Do not conform to the pattern of this world, but be transformed by the renewing of your mind"* (Rom. 12:2). Aligning with worldly values and the spirit of the age results in falling under the influence of disobedience and sin.

9. *Lack of Discernment:*

- *"Be very careful, then, how you live — not as unwise but as wise, making the most of every opportunity, because the days are evil"* (Eph.5:15-16). Living without careful consideration and ignoring God's Word leads to true foolishness and a wasted life.

10. *Rejection of Truth:*

- *"They perish because they refused to love the truth and so be saved. For this reason God sends them a powerful delusion so that they will believe the lie and so that all will be condemned who have not believed the truth but have delighted in wickedness"* (2Thess.2:10-12).Disregard for the truth and delighting in wickedness results in believing lies and condemnation.

From the scriptural references, it is evident that the causes of falling into the evil actions of the old self are fundamentally connected to knowledge and understanding. Whether through arrogance, rejection, neglect, or ignorance of the truth, sin is inherently linked to how we perceive and respond to God's will and truth.

Second Type, The Positive Type: The practices of the new self, particularly consistent prayer and praise, are central to Christian life. Regular gatherings of believers for prayer and praise represent a profound and continuous communion with the risen Christ. This is not a mere intellectual or abstract connection but a tangible, holistic interaction with Christ, allowing Him to deeply integrate into our reality. This connection isn't just about being with Him; it's about Him being with us according to His divine will: *"For where two or three gather in my name, there am I with them"* (Matt.18:20).

The good works prepared by the Lord act as daily spiritual nourishment from heaven, working invisibly and profoundly within our new creation. These works strengthen the new members of the body and unify them, providing the entire body with love, joy, and inspiration, thus reflecting a renewed power and unity in the Spirit: *"If one part suffers, every part suffers with it; if one part is honoured, every part rejoices with it"* (1 Cor.12:26). Each individual benefits from this fullness, which grows as God's new gifts are poured out upon the whole body: *"Now you are the body of Christ, and each one of you is a part of it"* (1 Cor.12:27).

Ultimately, each person, embodying the new self, shares in the honour and glory of the body, reflecting the dignity and glory of Christ. This unity is a manifestation of love, sacrifice, harmony, and compassion, leading to the glorification of God: *"I have given them the glory that you gave me, that they may be one as we are one... I in them and you in me"* (John.17:22-23).

But, How Good Works Glorify God When Christ said, *"Let your light shine before others, that they may see your good deeds and glorify your Father in heaven"*

(Matt.5:16), He meant that the divine light reflected through good works reveals God's glory to the world. The material and logical world cannot know God on its own: "*The person without the Spirit does not accept the things that come from the Spirit of God but considers them foolishness, and cannot understand them because they are discerned only through the Spirit. The person with the Spirit makes judgments about all things, but such a person is not subject to merely human judgments*" (1 Cor.2:14-15).

Knowledge of God requires the Holy Spirit, who reveals the connection between the Creator and creation. Without the Holy Spirit, the natural world and its logic cannot grasp this connection: "*The Spirit of truth, whom the world cannot accept because it neither sees nor knows him. But you know him, for he lives with you and will be in you*" (John.14:17).

Thus, good works performed through the Holy Spirit and by the new self- created anew through resurrection are the sole bridge between the material world and God. These works, achieved by grace, serve as the only spiritual proof of God as Creator and reveal His hidden power behind nature. They are the primary means of glorifying God. For these works to fully achieve their purpose, they must unite the disparate parts into one cohesive body that acts miraculously beyond natural levels, characterized by love, fellowship, sacrifice, and redemption. The church, as a unified and grateful entity, becomes a living testament to God's existence, work, and goodness, serving as a miracle in the new world and glorifying God eternally.

However, the church's witness to God as a new creation is often compromised by divisions and conflicts, whether doctrinal, denominational, or material. The world remains distant from God because the church, in its fragmented and temporal state, fails to represent Him accurately. This fragmentation and focus on material concerns detract from the essence of good works, making the church's actions appear as mere earthly behaviour. Consequently, the church's division undermines its role as a living witness to God, inadvertently demonstrating to the world the absence of God.

CHAPTER FIVE

BAPTISM AND THE NEW CREATION: UNVEILING TRANSFORMATION AND SON-SHIP

Baptism as the Gateway to the New Creation

Christ was the first to reveal the profound mystery of baptism and firmly link it to the Kingdom of God. When Nicodemus came to Jesus at night in Jerusalem, seeking to understand the Kingdom Jesus was preaching, Jesus responded: *"Very truly I tell you, no one can see the Kingdom of God unless they are born again"* (John.3:3). This statement is deeply profound: only those who are born from above can perceive the higher spiritual realities. Nicodemus, confused by the idea of being born again, thought Jesus meant a physical rebirth. Jesus then clarified: *"Very truly I tell you, no one can enter the Kingdom of God unless they are born of water and the Spirit"* (John.3:5). This too is a profound truth, as the Kingdom of God is spiritual and can only be entered by those born of the Spirit. To prevent Nicodemus from misunderstanding this as a physical process, Jesus added: *"Flesh gives birth to flesh, but the Spirit gives birth to spirit"* (John.3:6). Here, Jesus is pointing to a new spiritual birth distinct from the old physical one. The first birth grants a physical body, while the second birth provides a spiritual nature. The physical body, being made from dust, is ultimately inconsequential for the Kingdom of God, as it returns to the earth with death. In contrast, the new spiritual self, born of the Holy Spirit and water, is a heavenly being, created to see and enter the Kingdom of God and to live within it.

Thus, Jesus described baptism as the gateway to heaven through which those born of water and the Spirit may enter.

Baptism is the foremost and most significant sacrament in the Church. The Church alone has been entrusted with this sacrament, as it is considered to be carrying out and advancing the work of the Kingdom of God on earth, just as it has been entrusted with the Holy Spirit and the dispensation of spiritual gifts. It is both the right and the duty of the Church to bring forth children for Christ, members of the Kingdom. Since it is clear that without being born from above, one cannot see the Kingdom, and without being born of water and the Spirit, one cannot enter it, it follows that the Church holds the key to the mystery of entering the Kingdom of God through baptism. Through baptism, a person is spiritually reborn, becoming a new creation who awaits the day when the old self will be cast aside to fully embrace the Kingdom of God.

The new self, born through baptism and created spiritually from above, does not exist in isolation under the influence of the old self. Instead, because it is born from the nature of Christ, who is risen from the dead, it remains in constant and intimate connection with Him. Only sin, such as the denial of Christ as the Son of God who became incarnate, was crucified, and rose again, can sever this connection. As the Apostle John writes: *"If anyone acknowledges that Jesus is the Son of God, God lives in them and they in God. So we have come to know and to believe the love God has for us. God is love. Whoever lives in love lives in God, and God in them"* (1 John.4:15-16). *"Who is the liar? It is whoever denies that Jesus is the Christ. Such a person is the antichrist—denying the Father and the Son"* (1 John.2:22). *"And now, dear children, continue in him, so that when he appears we may be confident and unashamed before him at his coming"* (1 John.2:28).

Thus, the new self in baptism bears the image and nature of Christ, as affirmed by Paul: *"For we are God's handiwork, created in Christ Jesus to do good works, which God prepared in advance for us to do"* (Eph.2:10). *"Put on the new self, created to be like God in true righteousness and holiness"* (Eph.4:24). *"For all of you who were baptized into Christ have clothed yourselves with Christ"* (Gal.3:27). This indicates a state of on-going existence and unity with Christ, as Paul describes: *"But whoever is united with the Lord is one with him in spirit"* (1 Cor.6:17). John refers to this as a continual spiritual fellowship with the Father and His Son Jesus Christ. These scriptures illustrate that baptism creates a new internal and spiritual reality within the individual, embodying the image of God and the nature of resurrection in Christ, a state that is free from the dominion of death and is prepared for eternal elevation.

Baptism as the Mystical Death of the Old Self

Baptism signifies the mystical death of the old self and its deeds. In the theology of the Church, baptism is not just a symbolic act but a profound participation in Christ's death on the cross and His burial for three days, symbolized by three immersions in the name of the Father, the Son, and the Holy Spirit. As stated in Romans 6:4, *"We were therefore buried with him through baptism into death, in order that, just as Christ was raised from the dead through the glory of the Father, we too may live a new life."*

It's important to understand that baptism, through faith, involves a genuine spiritual union with Christ in His suffering, crucifixion, death, and resurrection. When an individual is immersed in water, it represents a complete renunciation of worldly ways and sins. Publicly rejecting Satan signifies a personal commitment and covenant. Being submerged three times symbolizes participation in Christ's death, His descent into the tomb, and the fulfilment of the penalty for sin.

This is not just a ritual devoid of real significance; rather, it represents a true act of will parallel to Christ's suffering and death. Christ's actions on the cross and in the tomb are divine acts completed by the Son of God, made available to believers through faith. The power of baptism mirrors the power of Christ's sacrifice on the cross for all who believe. Even though Christ, being sinless, did not need to die, He submitted to the Father's will to redeem humanity from sin and death. Thus, those who believe and affirm their faith through baptism become participants in these divine acts and receive their benefits.

Baptism involves shedding the old self, as Paul explains: "*In him you were also circumcised, with a circumcision not performed by human hands, but with the circumcision of Christ, having been buried with him in baptism, in which you were also raised with him through your faith in the working of God, who raised him from the dead. When you were dead in your sins and in the uncircumcision of your flesh, God made you alive with Christ. He forgave us all our sins*" (Col.2:11-13).

Paul compares the removal of the old self in baptism to Jewish circumcision, which symbolizes purification and cleansing. Therefore, baptism, akin to circumcision, represents a total removal of the old self and its deeds. This process is referred to as "*the body of the sins of the flesh,*" accomplished through our union with Christ's death and burial: "*Buried with him in baptism*" signifies our belief that in baptism, we share in Christ's crucifixion and death.

This theological truth is affirmed by Paul: "*If Christ is in you (through baptism), even though your body is subject to death because of sin, the Spirit gives life because of righteousness (the righteousness of God in Christ), which He granted us through His resurrected body*" (Rom.8:10). *Additionally,* "*Because through Christ Jesus the law of the Spirit who gives life has set you free from the law of sin and death*" (Rom.8:2).

Paul the Apostle speaks directly to believers in Christ who, through baptism, have shed their old selves burdened by sin and the law's judgment of death, and have embraced their new spiritual selves. He says: "*You, however, are not in the flesh (the old self) but in the Spirit (the new self), if indeed the Spirit of God dwells in you*" (Rom.8:9). This indicates that the act of removing the old self with its deeds is essentially the work Christ accomplished on the cross and in the tomb for us. We receive this new self through faith and baptism, symbolized by immersion in water.

Paul clarifies that we have been liberated from the law of sin and death that once dominated our old selves. Even though sin may still influence the old self, it has no power over the new spiritual self we gain through baptism. This new self is seen as having been resurrected with Christ, overcoming sin in preparation for ascending to heaven, where it inherits eternal life with Christ who resides within. Paul emphasizes this truth by stating: "*There is now no condemnation for those who are in Christ Jesus*" (Rom.8:1). This refers to those who, through baptism, have left behind their old selves with its sinful deeds and embraced the new self, which is a new creation in the image of its Creator, characterized by righteousness and holiness.

The Revelation of Sons-hip to the New Man in Baptism

When Christ was baptized, God the Father declared from heaven, "*This is My beloved Son, in whom I am well pleased*" (Matt.3:17). Likewise, those born of God through water and the Spirit receive a witness from the Spirit within them: "*For you did not receive a spirit of bondage again to fear, but you received the Spirit of adoption by whom we cry out, 'Abba, Father!' The Spirit Himself bears witness with our spirit that we are children of God*" (Rom.8:15-16). James further explains, "*Of His own will He brought us forth by the word of truth, that we might be a kind of first fruits of His creatures*" (Jas.1:18). John adds, "*But as many as received Him, to them He gave the right to become children of God, to those who believe in His name, who were born, not of blood, nor of the will of the flesh, nor of the will of man, but of God*" (John.1:12-13).

The concept of being "*born again*" through the word of truth signifies a new creation established by God's word. Peter describes this new birth as a living hope: "*Blessed be the God and Father of our Lord Jesus Christ, who according to His abundant mercy has begotten us again to a living hope, through the resurrection of Jesus Christ from the dead*" (1 Peter.1:3). This "*new birth*" is a hope preserved in heaven. Peter also explains, "*Being born again, not of corruptible seed but incorruptible, through the word of God which lives and abides forever*" (1 Peter.1:23).

Peter's reference to the "*incorruptible seed*" symbolizes the Holy Spirit as the agent of spiritual rebirth, contrasting with the "*seed of man*" used for physical conception. John also emphasizes that the one born of God does not sin because God's seed remains in him (1 John.3:9). This means the Holy Spirit remains with the new man born through baptism, providing eternal life. Consequently, the new man lives by the Holy Spirit, and his life extends into eternity. *"As new born babes, desire the pure milk of the word, that you may grow thereby"* (1 Peter.2:2). The *"pure milk"* refers to the word of the Gospel, which we are to crave for spiritual growth, akin to a baby's desire for its mother's milk.

Therefore, *"putting on the new man"* involves a balanced process. As we shed the old self with its sinful actions, we are to embrace the new self with its good works, which God has prepared for us (Ephesians 2:10). Paul confirms this by saying, *"Therefore we do not lose heart. Even though our outward man is perishing, yet the inward man is being renewed day by day"* (2 Cor.4:16). This renewal is related to our awareness and struggle against the old self, which continually desires its own way. In the reality of God's work in baptism, the replacement is complete, as the creation of the new man in the Spirit is a one-time event that stands on its own. The individual is left only to explore the fullness of this magnificent work completed by God. God's gifts are perfect, and the new man is created in the image of his Creator, in righteousness and holiness. It is up to each person to believe and understand the truth of what God has done within them.

The scale of this work may be beyond human comprehension because it transcends human logic and merit. The creation of the new man is a divine act designed to transition humanity from earth to heaven and to live in God's Kingdom. It is a complete act of God's will: *"He willed to bring us forth by the word of truth that we might be a kind of first fruits of His creatures"* (Jas.1:18). The righteousness of God cannot be measured by our worthiness for this new creation. The sacrifice made by the Father and the suffering endured by the Son for our salvation and the gift of this new creation are beyond measure and understanding. What remains is to appreciate the value and grandeur of this new creation, surpassing all comprehension. The more we understand the greatness and glory of this work, the closer we come to grasping God's love and His glorious mystery. Ultimately, anyone who truly knows, believes in, and loves Christ will desire to draw nearer to Him, to sense His presence, and to hear His voice. But why?

Christ has inspired in us a profound longing for transformation. After revealing Himself as "*the Word*" who was with the Father and is the exact representation of God's essence — "*and the Word was God*" (John.1:1) — God allowed His Son to become incarnate. Born of a virgin, He became fully human, yet without sin. This profound act has stirred in us a deep desire to know Christ, our elder brother, to draw close to Him, and to see Him, for He embodies the mystery of God, His image, essence, and glory, while also embracing us.

Our yearning to know and connect with Christ intensifies because we understand that His incarnation was intended to lift the burden of the old self with its sins and failures — burdens that have weighed us down and led us to despair of living a life of holiness and righteousness before God. Therefore, truly knowing Christ and connecting with Him guarantees a life of holiness and righteousness, as He is the embodiment of holiness and justice.

In this context, being "*baptized into Christ*" signifies complete allegiance to Him. Baptism is viewed as a seal of total commitment to Christ. Spiritually, baptism symbolizes death — a full surrender of oneself as a living sacrifice. When we say "*baptized into Christ*," it means that this sacrifice is for Christ: "*we have died to Him*." This truth is revealed to us by God, without our prior questioning or understanding. After Christ completed His redemptive and atoning work on the cross and spent three days in the tomb to fulfils the penalty and curse of death, God raised Him from the dead, exalted Him above all heavens, and seated Him at His right hand. This was a perfect and comprehensive act to end our sins, lift the penalty of death and curse, and remove God's wrath from us. It granted us the status of children of God and an inheritance with Christ in His Kingdom and eternal life.

Despite this, humanity still needs to unite with Christ Himself to ensure that His redemptive and salvific work continues within us, along with His Spirit, righteousness, and grace. Through this union, we ensure the on-going removal of our old self that died with Him on the cross and the continuous wearing of the new self-created from His resurrected body and Spirit. This is precisely what God accomplished in us through the sacrament of baptism. He made our new spiritual self *"wear"* Christ the Lord, the Spirit, who is intrinsically connected to us because He created us in His image of righteousness and holiness.

Thus, wearing Christ signifies a union with the nature of the resurrected Christ, not merely acquiring His attributes. The new self draws from His inherent righteousness and holiness.

We might think that this is too grand and beyond human comprehension, but this is the gift of God and Christ. It must indeed be beyond ordinary logic and reason because God's greatness and Christ's greatness demand it. God's gifts are immense and boundless. As Paul describes the depth and scope of God's plan and His great gifts: *"Blessed be the God and Father of our Lord Jesus Christ, who has blessed us with every spiritual blessing in the heavenly places in Christ, just as He chose us in Him before the foundation of the world, that we should be holy and without blame before Him in love. Having predestined us to adoption as sons by Jesus Christ to Himself, according to the good pleasure of His will"* (Eph.1:3-5).

Thus, we should not be surprised when Paul says, *"I have been crucified with Christ; it is no longer I who live, but Christ lives in me. And the life which I now live in the flesh I live by faith in the Son of God, who loved me and gave Himself for me"* (Gal.2:20).

In this way, Christ fills our new self to the extent that we can truthfully say, *"Christ lives in me."* This represents a magnificent compensation according to God's grace and mercy—a dream of being cleansed from our old sinful self and clothed with a new self in the image of God, in righteousness and holiness. This is the essence of Christian faith! We are a new creation in Christ: *"Created in Christ Jesus for good works, which God prepared beforehand that we should walk in them"* (Eph.2:10).

If we question how the new self is created according to God in righteousness and holiness, the answer lies in the nature of God itself. The new creation is described as being *"according to God,"* in contrast to the old self, which is *"corrupt according to the deceitful lusts"* (Eph.4:22). This transformation occurs through the mystery of baptism, a profound process that happens beyond our conscious awareness, transcending our rational understanding and imagination. We only fully grasp this divine act of transformation when God reveals to us that we are a new creation according to His nature, in contrast to the *"old self, which is corrupt according to deceitful lusts."*

This process was accomplished in the Church through baptism, paralleling what Christ achieved on the cross, in the tomb, and through the resurrection. The mystery of baptism is supported by the power of Christ's death on the cross and His resurrection from the dead. Both of these operations are deeply mysterious and can only be understood through spiritual revelation. Thus, faith in Christ's death and resurrection is realized or made effective for the believer practically in the sacrament of baptism. In His death, Christ dealt with the body of sin and its corruption, and in His resurrection, He manifested righteousness, holiness, and eternal life: *"He was delivered up for our offenses, and was raised for our justification"* (Rom.4:25).

Through the new self within us, we automatically enter into fellowship with Christ: *"For as many of you as were baptized into Christ have put on Christ"* (Gal.3:27). This reveals the essence of Christian faith rather than merely its works. Belief in Christ as the Son of God, who came in the flesh, completed our redemption through His death on the cross, and secured salvation and eternal life through His resurrection, grants us the reality of fellowship with Christ through the sacrament of baptism. For both Paul and John, faith in Christ and the new creation through baptism represent the revelation of eternal life that was with the Father and manifested in Jesus. Thus, this revelation of eternal life, akin to the revelation of light, brings us into fellowship with Christ. Similarly, the revelation of truth — knowledge of it — places us in the truth, and the truth within us.

The grace of the revelation of eternal life in Christ naturally fosters fellowship with both Christ and the Father: *"The life was manifested (in Christ), and we have seen, and bear witness, and declare to you that eternal life which was with the Father and was manifested to us (in Christ). That which we have seen and heard we declare to you, that you also may have fellowship with us; and truly our fellowship is with the Father and with His Son Jesus Christ. And these things we write to you that your joy may be full"* (1 John.1:2-4). This is one of the greatest and most significant aspects of the Christian faith, available to everyone who believes with their heart and is baptized in the name of Christ.

How the New Self Is Free from Sin and Judgment

To understand why the new self does not sin and is exempt from judgment, we need to recognize that the new self, which is born again in the Spirit, shares its nature with the resurrected body of Christ. According to the Apostle John, this new self is inherently sinless and incapable of sinning: *"Everyone who is born of God does not sin because His seed remains in him; he cannot sin because he has been born of God"* (1 John.3:9).

The new self is spiritual: "Unless one is born of *water and the Spirit, he cannot enter the kingdom of God"* (John.3:5), and it is heavenly: *"Unless one is born from above, he cannot see the kingdom of God"* (John.3:3). Consequently, the inheritance of the new self, which is the kingdom of God, completely excludes any connection with the nature of sin, which pertains to the earthly body and ultimately returns to dust: *"For you are dust, and to dust you shall return"* (Gen.3:19).

John's clear view of the new self as sinless, due to its nature being created in the image of God in righteousness and holiness, contrasts with Paul's theological perspective. Paul describes the new self as having a spiritual nature that liberates a person from the old law, sin, and judgment. Therefore, the person who believes in Christ, is baptized, receives the anointing of the Holy Spirit, and becomes a new spiritual creation, is not subject to the judgment that will befall those who have not believed and continue to live in the old self, the self of sin. Paul says: *"For I delight in the law of God according to the inward man (the new spiritual self). But I see another law in my members (the old self) warring against the law of my mind (the new self- created according to God in righteousness and holiness), and bringing me into captivity to the law of sin which is in my members"* (Rom.7:22-23).

This presents a significant challenge for a Christian who has attained the new spiritual creation. The old body's desires and habits continue to act and intensify their assault on the new self, aiming to overpower it and impose the dominion of sin. Saint Paul, recognizing this struggle, exclaims: *"O wretched man that I am! Who will deliver me from this body of death?"* (Rom.7:24).

However, Paul's faith perspective brings clarity. He sees that God has not left him under the dominance of the old body and its sins dragging him into sin. Through Christ Jesus, God has provided another helper: a new creation in us from His Spirit and the resurrected body of Christ. This new self-overcomes sin, nullifies death and the law, and represents the *"new self-created in us according to God in righteousness and holiness."* This new self draws its law from the Spirit and Christ, performing righteousness for the sake of holiness and truth — not merely as attributes but as a nature sustained by God's grace. Paul recognizes this miraculous balance achieved through faith in Christ, where, in contrast to the old self's entrenched habits and sins, the new self, created with the nature of resurrection and the Spirit of God, triumphs in righteousness and holiness, overcoming the dominion of the old body. As Paul declares: *"I thank God through Jesus Christ our Lord! So then, with the mind I myself serve the law of God, but with the flesh the law of sin"* (Rom.7:25).
The result is: "There is therefore now no condemnation for those who are in Christ Jesus" (Rom.8:1) because: *"The law of the Spirit of life in Christ Jesus (which the*

new spiritual self in us was created in) has made me free from the law of sin and death" (Rom.8:2).

Here, the term *"made free"* contrasts with the previous *"brought into captivity."* Liberation from the law of sin comes not through human effort but through God's free gift of the new self -endowed with the law of the Spirit of life. Just as the old body, with its traits and habits, had the power to drag me into the law of sin, the law of the Spirit of life (grace) in Christ Jesus, which has taken root within me along with the new self, has a superior power to free me from the law of sin and death. This indicates that God has granted us this new spiritual body through faith in Christ and baptism, equipping us with its superior spiritual capabilities to nullify the dominance and tyranny of the old self in us, not just in our perceptions but before God's ultimate justice in righteousness and mercy.

Despite this, the greatest advantage we gain through Christian faith, by receiving the new self through faith and baptism, is that we are entirely exempt from the impending judgment: *"There is therefore now no condemnation for those who are in Christ Jesus."* This divine promise, while it is a free gift requiring no effort, often remains overlooked in teachings, with few recognizing its divine right. It is a free gift, echoing the Gospel promise: *"He who believes and is baptized will be saved"* (Mark.16:16), where belief must be from the heart.

The Relationship Between Baptism and the Cross

The Apostle Paul was among the first to highlight the central relationship between baptism and the cross. He writes: *"Or do you not know that as many of us as were baptized into Christ Jesus were baptized into His death? Therefore we were buried with Him through baptism into death, that just as Christ was raised from the dead by the glory of the Father, even so we also should walk in newness of life"* (Rom.6:3-4). This means that the mystery of baptism represents a profound participation and union with Christ. Through baptism, we are fully involved in His crucifixion, death, and burial, and consequently, we share in the results of these actions, which Paul immediately links to the resurrection: *"just as Christ was raised from the dead by the glory of the Father, even so we also should walk in newness of life."* By participating in His death and burial through baptism, we are entitled to share in His resurrection and live with Him in the new, eternal life.

But why was baptism given to us? Christ does not impart His suffering, death, and resurrection merely as a gift or a decree. The reality is profound and remarkable. Christ did not suffer and die for Himself, for He was without sin and had no connection to sin that would warrant punishment or death. Instead, by assuming our human nature through birth from the Virgin Mary and the Holy Spirit, He willingly submitted Himself to the Sanhedrin, accepted false accusations and an unjust trial, and did not defend Himself. By accepting these false charges and the subsequent punishment, He bore our sins in His body on the cross and died for them.

Thus, the sufferings He endured were truly our own, and His death and burial were, in essence, our own. His suffering, crucifixion, death, and burial were acts of participating in our punishment, or rather, we joined Him in our sinful nature so that, through His resurrection as the Son of God, He could raise us with Him, free from sin, without punishment or wrath, and reconcile us to God the Father in our new, created nature.

To convey this new sinless nature, freed from judgment, Christ established baptism as a spiritual mystery, through which this new nature is conferred upon us in the image of its Creator in righteousness and holiness. Baptism thus parallels all the redemptive acts performed by the Father in His Son, sharing in their efficacy, results, honour, and glory.

The verse before us reveals a profound and transformative truth: *"Or do you not know that as many of us as were baptized into Christ Jesus were baptized into His death? Therefore we were buried with Him through baptism into death, that just as Christ was raised from the dead by the glory of the Father, even so we also should walk in newness of life. For if we have been united together in the likeness of His death, certainly we also shall be in the likeness of His resurrection, knowing this, that our old man was crucified with Him, that the body of sin might be done away with, that we should no longer be slaves of sin. For he who has died has been freed from sin... For sin shall not have dominion over you, for you are not under law but under grace"* (Rom.6:3-7, 14).

In this passage, we discover that the essence of baptism is an active participation and union with Christ's death and resurrection. Through baptism, we are not merely symbolically but genuinely united with Christ's crucifixion, death, burial, and ultimately, His resurrection. By participating in His death and burial through baptism, we are granted the profound privilege of sharing in His resurrection, experiencing the newness of life that He secured for us.

However, the question arises: why has Christ given us this sacrament of baptism? It is crucial to understand that Christ did not simply offer His suffering and death as a mere gift or decree. The reality of His sacrifice is deep and astonishing. Christ, who had no sin of His own and was entirely innocent, took upon Himself our sins and our punishment. By assuming our human nature and accepting unjust judgment, He bore our guilt and the penalty we deserved. Thus, His suffering and death were not His own but ours. He accepted our sins and, through His death, paid the full penalty.

Consequently, the suffering, death, and burial endured by Christ were, in essence, our own. Just as Christ's death brought about redemption and freedom from sin, so too does baptism effectuate this same freedom. Through baptism, the old self, which was crucified with Christ, is symbolically and spiritually put to death. In the same way, we receive freedom from sin and are justified through this sacrament. As Christ's body was raised with the Father's glory and righteousness after death and burial, so through baptism, we receive the power of His resurrection, emerging justified and blameless before Him in love and grace.

Furthermore, Paul emphasizes in his letter to the Ephesians that all the benefits of Christ's suffering, death, burial, resurrection, ascension, and exaltation—such as the subjugation of all heavenly powers—are granted to us through the Church: *"And what is the exceeding greatness of His power toward us who believe, according to the working of His mighty power which He worked in Christ when He raised Him from the dead and seated Him at His right hand in the heavenly places, far above all principality and power and might and dominion, and every name that is named, not only in this age but also in that which is to come. And He put all things under His feet, and gave Him to be head over all things to the church, which is His body, the fullness of Him who fills all in all"* (Eph.1:19-23).

Thus, all the gains achieved through Christ's death and resurrection are bestowed upon the Church and, by extension, upon us. The core of redemption and atonement was Christ's death of the sinful self and the emergence of the new spiritual self. This is precisely what baptism signifies: the removal of the old man who was crucified and died with Christ, and the clothing of the new man, created in God's image in righteousness and holiness, which is Christ Himself. This sacrament, profound in its mystery, symbolizes the greatest acts of faith. It is administered freely and secretly through baptism, making one a new creation to live with Christ in the newness of life—an eternal life in full and intimate communion with Christ through the Holy Spirit.

Therefore, the ritual of baptism stresses the necessity of shedding garments that symbolize the old self and entering the water completely naked, representing burial. This occurs three times in the name of the Holy Trinity. Upon emerging from the water, the individual is clothed in a new white robe, symbolizing the new self. While these actions are symbolic, they have profound divine significance and reflect the realities of the cross. Just as Christ's death and resurrection revealed the ultimate act of redemption, baptism reveals the death of the old self and the clothing of the new spiritual self. Thus, faith in the cross and resurrection is inherently linked to faith in baptism, sharing the same power and efficacy, rooted in the belief in God's revelation through both the cross and baptism. This understanding is realized through the spiritual awareness of the new self.

The Awareness of the New Man Rooted in Faith, Hope, and Love

The function of awareness in the new man—an enlightened mind—is to maintain a profound connection with his Creator. This connection is realized through three essential gifts that facilitate union with God and Christ:

First: The foremost power of awareness in the new man is faith, which hinges on the acceptance of divine revelations. Faith instils an immediate sense of God's righteousness in the new self, similar to how a child feels a personal bond with his father. When one embraces with faith the truth that God loves us and has revealed eternal life through His Son, the direct reward from God is this very eternal life, and the gift of His Son Himself. This bestows upon us a new life in Him and grants us the privilege of being united with the Father: *"Our fellowship is with the Father and with His Son Jesus Christ"* (1 John.1:3). This union comes as a result of our belief in the Father's love and His gift of eternal life through His Son.

Second: The second power of awareness for the new man is hope. Hope provides us with confidence in God and anticipation of His promises as though they have already been fulfilled. This certainty ensures that our rights are secured and allows us to experience a foretaste of these promises, elevating our joy in God to unparalleled heights: *"Rejoicing in hope"* (Rom.12:12).

Third: The third power of awareness for the new man is love. Love enables us to see God as the supreme and most significant presence in our lives, causing our own selves to fade into the background. In this way, God's presence is evident in us while we remain unseen. His name becomes our most treasured gift, and He rewards us with a love that surpasses description, akin to the Father's love for the Son: *"He who loves Me will be loved by My Father, and I will love him and manifest Myself to him"* (John.14:21). Love, originating from God, indicates that everyone who loves is born of God and knows God (1 John.4:7).

The impact of these three spiritual forces — faith, hope, and love — on the new man is profound. They enable the Christian to grow in the knowledge of God, His love, and His obedience without obstruction, fostering complete submission and adherence. By utilizing the gifts of faith, hope, and love bestowed by God, the new man becomes sanctified and becomes a cherished possession of God, not through his own actions but through the inherent power and gifts within him.

These three virtues — faith, hope, and love — are intrinsic to the nature of the new man, preparing him for an eternal fellowship with God. While love is the greatest, faith serves as the gateway to the profound mysteries and gifts of God, as *"without faith it is impossible to please Him"* (Heb.11:6). It is difficult to isolate any one of these virtues. Faith, hope, and love form a triangular grace with its apex directed upward, each side converging at a single focal point — the eye of spiritual perception.

Chapter Six.

The New Baptismal Identity: Revealing the Resurrection and Redemption.

The New Baptismal Man, the Church, and the Body of Christ

The rebirth of man through water and the Spirit — baptism, as Christ described — is a profound and mystical extension of Christ's resurrection, transforming the human body into a glorified, spiritually renewed state. Through this sacrament, death's penalty is lifted, and triumph over sin and Satan is achieved. The spiritually renewed individual, now a new creation in Christ, becomes an active and vital member of the Church, which, through him, embodies the resurrected and united Body of Christ.

Saint Paul, inspired by the Spirit, vividly describes this connection between the baptized individual and the Church: *"Christ also loved the Church and gave Himself for her, that He might sanctify and cleanse her with the washing of water by the word, that He might present her to Himself a glorious Church, not having spot or wrinkle or any such thing, but that she should be holy and without blemish"* (Eph.5:25-27). Paul also describes the baptized individual with similar attributes: *"And such were some of you. But you were washed, but you were sanctified, but you were justified in the name of the Lord Jesus and by the Spirit of our God"* (1 Cor.6:11). This indicates that Paul sees the new spiritual Church as the embodiment of the baptized individual.

Thus, when Paul asserts that *"the Church is the Body of Christ,"* he is not merely referring to a concept but rather encapsulating the true nature of the Church and the Body of Christ. The relationship between the Church and the Body of Christ is strikingly illustrated in baptism: *"For as many of you as were baptized into Christ have put on Christ"* (Gal.3:27). In baptism, each believer is enveloped in Christ, meaning that Christ becomes the source of their new life, enlightenment, and truth. This transformation led Saint Paul to declare: *"It is no longer I who live, but Christ lives in me"* (Gal.2:20). Paul's emphasis on *"I"* signifies that it is not the self that provides new life, but Christ who becomes the central identity in us—the new man—uniting Christians as a single entity with Christ.

To dispel any superficial or theoretical understanding of the new man created in Christ's image, Paul asserts: *"For we are members of His body, of His flesh and of His bones"* (Eph.5:30). This affirmation clarifies the essence of the new man in baptism, forming the foundation of the Church. To understand our true connection to Christ's resurrected body, consider Christ's entrance into the locked room and His appearance among the terrified disciples, who initially mistook Him for a spirit. He reassured them: *"Handle Me and see, for a spirit does not have flesh and bones as you see I have"* (Luke 24:39).

Therefore, Christ's resurrection was in His body, with flesh and bones, though in a state of glorification that is not visible or tangible unless revealed by the Lord. This glorified state allowed the disciples to perceive and touch Him spiritually and believe. In this definitive and confirmed reality, we are formed in baptism into a new spiritual existence from Christ's flesh and bones, embodying a glorified and transcendent state. Saint Paul's assertion, *"For we are members of His body, of His flesh and of His bones,"* speaks of our new creation in baptism, granting us an invisible yet real membership in His resurrected body.

Thus, humanity is prepared to be united with its heavenly Bridegroom as a justified spiritual creation, bringing joy to God's heart. As flesh and bones of the resurrected Christ, we are spiritually transformed and ready for glory. Christ, as the new Adam, is the Father of the new creation, and we are His creation: *"Created in Christ Jesus for good works, which God prepared beforehand that we should walk in them"* (Eph.2:10).

The Resurrection Image of Christ in Our New Bodies

We now bear the image of the resurrected Christ in our new bodies, not merely in appearance but in the essence of holiness and righteousness: *"And put on the new man which was created according to God, in true righteousness and holiness"* (Eph.4:24). This underscores that these attributes are inherent to the new nature that Christ assumed in His resurrection — a nature free from death and corruption, entirely detached from the old law and earthly elements. This nature now qualifies us for eternal life, which we experience as a foretaste through our spiritual union with Christ, until the moment we shed our old, earthly body.

Saint Paul vividly describes the nature and depth of our relationship with Christ: *"For in Him dwells all the fullness of the Godhead bodily. And you are complete in Him, who is the head of all principality and power"* (Col.2:9-10). *"In Him you were also circumcised with the circumcision made without hands, by putting off the body of the sins of the flesh, by the circumcision of Christ. Buried with Him in baptism, in which you also were raised with Him through faith in the working of God, who raised Him from the dead. And you, being dead in your trespasses and the un-circumcision of your flesh, He has made alive together with Him, having forgiven you all trespasses"* (Col.2:11-13).

From these passages, we discern that the new man's nature encompasses the fullness of Christ's divine body. Whereas we were once filled with sin, deceit, iniquity, and worldly desires, we are now spiritually filled with what pertains to Christ. This highlights the immense value of the new birth through water and the Spirit, which has endowed us with the fullness of Christ, the Son of God, and a nature that is heavenly in origin. Thus, we have definitively departed from our former earthly nature.

Paul describes the removal of the old human body through Christ's death as a metaphorical circumcision—an unparalleled and creative analogy. We are, therefore, circumcised in Christ, meaning the old body has been spiritually removed by grace. This represents the true purification of the New Covenant. Purification in the New Testament means the removal of the old body's deeds: *"How much more shall the blood of Christ, who through the eternal Spirit offered Himself without spot to God, cleanse your conscience from dead works (the deeds of the old, dead body) to serve the living God"* (Heb.9:14).

We see that we have been united with Christ's death through the sacrament of baptism, being buried in water and then raised with Him as a new creation, having shed the body of human sin. This union is based on our firm belief in His death and resurrection on our behalf. Through baptism, we receive the reality of His resurrection in our new selves and are forgiven all the sins of the old man, which have been erased permanently by God's unregretful actions.

Christ Himself, through His suffering, wounds, cross, and death, has removed the old body with its sins and the judgment of death against it, burying it in the past, never to return. He has raised us with Him, both in His resurrection and through our baptism, establishing the new creation. This new creation manifests in the visible action of the cross and the profound sacrament of baptism. Christ has traversed death, hell, and the abyss with us, delivering us with immense power and glory that was unattainable through our own means.

Christ first took our body from the Virgin and the Holy Spirit, pure and holy. Yet, He had to bear our sins on the cross, a task that terrified Him more than death itself. He struggled with His Father to pass this cup of human sins, distinct from the cup of death. While He willingly accepted death, the cup of humanity's sins posed an unfathomable challenge. How could He, the sinless Son, stand before His Father with humanity's transgressions? The Father's relationship with the Son is one of absolute holiness and unbreakable love. This conflict surpassed all wisdom, resolved only by the Son's submission to the Father's will: *"Not My will, but Yours be done"* (Luke.22:42). The Father's will was for the Son to bear human shame and all our sins, a price of the utmost gravity.

The Redemption Through Christ's Suffering and Resurrection

Christ approached the high priests with a resolve to endure the shame and accusations levelled against Him, including blasphemy, which He accepted without argument. When He was handed over to

Pilate, He faced additional charges—being a doer of evil, misleading the nation, and violating the law and the temple. He accepted these charges without defence, leading to the judgment of crucifixion. Bearing all accusations as truth, He was nailed to the cross, carrying not only the sins but also the curse of the cross as a condemned criminal. In this way, it is said that He "*bore our sins!*" He willingly embraced death as the penalty for the sins He took upon Himself, identifying Himself with the sinner. Our sin was His sin, our shame was His shame, and our death was His penalty. Upon His resurrection, having fulfilled the penalty for humanity's sins, He raised us with Him in His resurrection body, free from sin, death, and curse. Through baptism, He imparted to us a body of resurrection, justified by His obedience and triumph over death. This is the essence of redemption.

Christ did not merely die for us; He died with us, bearing our sinful body and its penalties. He took our death upon Himself out of profound love, honour, and obedience to His Father. In doing so, He died and rose for us, granting us the power of His death to overcome sin and death and the power of His resurrection to live anew. This is redemption! By His death, He freed us from the grip of death, and through His resurrection, He saved us from corruption. He lifted our shame and curse by His crucifixion, fulfilling the penalties imposed upon us with His own body, overcoming them with His divine holiness and profound son-ship. He rose with strength, glory, and victory. This is redemption.

Had He not died with us, we would have been forever consumed by death with no escape. Had He not risen, we would have been forever ravaged by corruption with no hope. And had it not been for His divine power, we would have been lost to the abyss, descending into hell with no hope of return. This is redemption. He paid the price for our sins through scourging, mocking, spitting, and the crown of thorns—each act a further indignity and disgrace. Thus, He completed our chastisement, allowing us to receive forgiveness of sins. He tasted the bitterness of death so that we might experience the victory of life. This is redemption.

We were under divine wrath due to disobedience, with no mediator until the only Son came, donning our disobedience as a garment and entering judgment fully aware of the cost. When Christ was raised on the cross, the Father's face was turned away, and He tasted the bitterness of divine wrath. Unable to bear it, He cried out: *"My God, My God, why have You forsaken Me?"* (Matthew 27:46). This cry was our own, as humanity entered a moment of darkness. Christ voiced it with our own words to declare that judgment had been fulfilled and that He bore divine wrath on our behalf. He was heard due to His reverence and obedience, even unto death as a sacrificial lamb. Without being the only Son, we would never have emerged from divine wrath. Thus, Christ achieved reconciliation for us after enduring shame, terror, and blood, bringing us into divine sonship. This is redemption.

Now, we see the immense cost to God and Christ for creating this new man—a spiritual rebirth made in His image, crafted in the nature of His resurrection body, and formed in righteousness and holiness. The price was extraordinarily high because it involved a nature superior in essence, safeguarded from death and corruption, supported by grace, and upheld by Christ's righteousness and holiness. This new nature, loved by Christ as a bridegroom loves his bride, represents our new creation. It is of His flesh and bones, and thus, our new nature is the very body of Christ, with Him as its head, inseparably united, seated at the right hand of the Father— a position He secured with His blood and prepared for us through His Spirit. This is the core of Christian faith, the truth of our Christianity, which bestowed this new creation freely, untouched by sin, death, or hell, fortified by the grace of resurrection to live triumphantly with righteousness inherited from Christ's resurrection.

When the old flesh unjustly exerts its power over us and grieves our souls through weakness or sin, we must remain vigilant. This is a cunning deception of the devil, for the old flesh is dead and its deeds are lifeless. These deeds are fully recognized before God and will disappear instantly. The sins of the old flesh no longer hold the power and dominion they once did because all our sins have been covered by the official pardon through the blood of Christ. These sins cannot affect our relationship with God and Christ, nor can they alter our heavenly inheritance unless we willingly forsake our heavenly portion and disregard the sacrifice of Christ.

As Christian believers, we need to grasp our new status before God as new creations, secured from falling, and victorious over death, sin, and the abyss. We should never underestimate our rights, for the price of our redemption was paid by God Himself. Nothing on earth or in heaven can snatch us from the grasp of God and Christ. We are encouraged to lift our heads high because, through our new identity as believers who have embraced redemption, we rise above death, sin, the abyss, and this world. No force in existence can separate us from the love of Christ, who has redeemed us with His blood.

Yet, it is essential to understand redemption on a personal and experiential level. Redemption remains a theoretical concept and a truth affirmed through baptism and faith until we accept the crucified and risen Christ deeply within our lives, leading to a real transformation. When we clearly experience this change in our lives, that is redemption in action!

Redemption is the work of Christ that ultimately settles in our lives, allowing us to begin our journey in Christ, experience all the promises of the Gospel, and look forward with confidence to a blessed future. Everything we have received from Christ, settled into our new lives, our love for Him, the changes we have undergone since knowing Him, and the principles we now live by, along with the joy and peace we experience — this constitutes our new self. In essence, our new self -embodies the transformation that has occurred within us.

The Apostle Paul clarifies the relationship between redemption and salvation in this verse: "*If you declare with your mouth, 'Jesus is Lord,' and believe in your heart that God raised Him from the dead, you will be saved. For it is with your heart that you believe and are justified, and it is with your mouth that you profess your faith and are saved*" (Rom.10:9-10). Belief in the heart represents the work of the new self, where faith stems from union with Christ. Believing in the resurrection of Jesus is a faith in the work of redemption. When the new self-embraces redemption by faith, it completes the salvation from the old self, its deeds, and the associated wrath. Faith and the reception of redemption come first in the heart, and the confession of salvation follows with the mouth, as a result of this redemption.

Chapter Seven.

The New Self in Christ : Defining Traits and the Return to a New Heart

How to Embrace the New Self

After delving into the concept of the new creation within us, the pressing question now is: How do I engage with my new self? How can I strive to be *"perfect,"* as God first instructed Abraham: *"Walk before Me and be perfect"* (Gen.17:1)? This was God's initial commandment, a foundational principle we should both hear and follow, as it pertains directly to our lives. When we begin to move away from past foolishness and youthful impulsiveness, cease trivial actions, and start to speak with wisdom and make decisions with prudence, we may feel a divine strength supporting and encouraging us, as though heaven itself is our ally.

Yet, the remarkable truth is that this support and strength originate from within—from the heart and from the new self that emerges as we strive to manifest Christ within us. When others observe the refinement and wisdom developing in us, they might mistakenly view it as self-aggrandizement or even call it *"superhuman"* wisdom. However, the reality is that we have simply discovered our true selves, created by God in righteousness and holiness. This new self, with its divine gifts, begins to shine through, bringing qualities that transcend ordinary human nature. The gifts inherent in our new self are wholly celestial; when they are expressed, they naturally elevate us beyond our previous limits.

This new power has the ability to suppress the old self, forcing it to retreat and making room for the new self to assert its divine presence. As the old self is confined and pushed back, its desires wane, and its shortcomings become evident, signalling the onset of the new self's role in service to God and eternity.

Such transformation might require significant effort and struggle, sustained by perseverance, heartfelt prayers filled with tears, pain, and sorrow — a process akin to a profound labour. It involves the death of the old self, which resists tenaciously, and the birth of the new self, which represents a substantial shift as it is reborn in the image of its Creator in righteousness and holiness. The forces driving the expulsion of the old self and the emergence of the new self- surpass our human capacity, as we seem to work against our own nature, almost as if we are dying to ourselves. Without the genuine competence of the new self, truly created in the image of its Creator, this transformation would be difficult or even impossible. But God created it to live and thrive without barriers to its rightful existence. The vitality of the new self - overcomes the works of the old self with triumphant force, leaving us amazed at the newfound support and wondering why it seemed hidden before, as if it were imprisoned. We begin to sense a call from within, as if an inner voice is urging us to move forward.

This transformation might also occur suddenly, as experienced by many, without extended struggle or effort. It can feel like awakening from a deep slumber, where the new self is on the brink of emergence, awaiting divine grace at the moment of fervent faith. The person then appears visibly renewed, becoming a subject of curiosity and wonder. It is said that someone has been transformed or changed, and they feel within themselves, in their voice, demeanour, smile, and serene joy, a clear and profound new beginning. Their calmness permeates their entire life, signalling a true spiritual rebirth where new spiritual energies flow into them, seemingly coming from above, yet originating from within, from the essence of their being and their heavenly inheritance

A Defining Trait of the New Self

Whether the transformation into a new self — truly becoming a new creation — comes through persistent effort, hardship, prayer, and perseverance, or through a sudden, dramatic change, we find that the conditions and experiences of the new self are remarkably similar across different individuals. Essentially, the new self universally reflects a spiritual image of Christ, as the Apostle Paul described: "*all have put on Christ.*" This new self is characterized by simplicity, joy, wisdom, inspiration, grace, heightened awareness, and spiritually impactful speech, which are common traits among those who have embraced and lived out their new identity.

This is a true testament to the reality of the second birth from above, which Christ has introduced to our world. His coming, incarnation, and the redemption He accomplished through His suffering, crucifixion, sacrifice, death, and resurrection represent a comprehensive and complete transformation of humanity into a new spiritual creation from above, preparing us for the divine transition into eternal life with God.

Thus, we see, feel, believe, and testify to the new creation we received secretly through baptism. It was hidden in our hearts until we reached a state of readiness to fully accept it. When we called it forth, it came into existence, visible for all to see and witness its truth. Through this new creation, the true Church—possessing these once-hidden gifts—becomes evident. It is revealed in all who have received the grace to reclaim their new spiritual creation. You are invited to join these individuals, adorned with Christ, to become a bride radiant with the glory of the Son.

Returning to the New Heart

With spiritual insight, we recognize that the new heart holds the key to the true door and path. As the Apostle Paul expressed, *"For as many of you as were baptized into Christ have put on Christ"* (Gal.3:27). If Christ is truly present in the new spiritual self, then within this self lies the key to both the door and the path. It is within this new self that genuine encounters, unions, and fellowship with Christ take place, resulting in *"complete joy"* (1 John.1:4). Is not eternal life itself present within us? If we have welcomed the presence of Christ, we have also embraced eternal life and fellowship with the Father and His Son, Jesus Christ. John's testimony affirms this reality: *"The life was manifested, and we have seen it, and bear witness, and declare to you that eternal life, which was with the Father and was manifested to us. That which we have seen and heard we declare to you, that you also may have fellowship with us; and truly our fellowship is with the Father and with His Son Jesus Christ. And these things we write to you that your joy may be full"* (1 John 1:2-4). Here, the truth of our Lord Jesus' words is fulfilled: "*The kingdom of God is within you*" (Luke. 17:21).

Thus, finding Christ, the kingdom, or eternal life is not achieved through mere intellectual effort, study, or striving. This has been a maze we have navigated for centuries, and now it is time to understand that Christ resides within us and eternal life is in our hearts. So, what should we do? We should focus our faith, prayer, and hope on the heart, for it is there that the new self, the new creation from above, is revealed. This new self has received the presence of Christ, the Spirit, and eternal life. Those who have discovered their new- self have found redemption, salvation, and eternal life, fulfilling everything required by God. God has implanted in our hearts the mystery of the new creation, complete with all its gifts and blessings. How rich and glorious this is!

There is no longer a need for blame, lamentation, or complaint. God has never been lacking in His care for us. He has not left us to face life with our old, flawed, and earthly bodies. God was not unjust in demanding the heavenly from us while we were equipped only with our broken, earthly tools. He did not ask us to know, believe, obey, or love Him with our corrupt, limited earthly capacities. Nor did He demand constant prayer and vigilance with our fragile, earthly instruments. Nor did He expect us to love our brothers from a pure heart or to love our enemies with a love limited to earthly instincts. Instead, and this is a true testimony, He has graciously given us a completely new human creation, not made from earthly dust, but a heavenly creation resembling the resurrected body of Christ — one that overcame sin, defeated death, and vanquished Satan, ascending from the realm of decay and destruction. This new creation comes with all spiritual gifts, the weapons of grace, the spirit of prayer, divine love, and childlike humility.

Christ has equipped us with His body, spirit, and love, and has entrusted this new creation to our hearts, sealed until the day we fully recognize and embrace it. In doing so, He has provided us with more than He demands. We are no longer strangers to the Father; heaven is no longer distant with Christ within us. It has become our home, awaiting us with more than we can imagine, and our inheritance is secure.

The reality is now clear. God did not create us to dwell in these old, failing bodies, lamenting our past and wasted time on false pursuits, suffering from forgiven shortcomings, or grieving our inability to fulfils His commandments. We should not idealize saints while despising our own days that have passed without bearing fruit or offering it to God. We should not mourn our death and the deaths of loved ones, enveloped in despair. The Gospel's statement that *"corruption cannot inherit in-corruption"* stands as a testimony against our misconceptions. This truth is reserved solely for those who possess the new self and the new creation whose true homeland is heaven. Thus, we squander our lives in vain while, if we lift our eyes, we would find living examples of new life. These individuals, who have transitioned from the old, dead works of the earthly body to the new, spiritual body, exhibit the characteristics of Christ and bear witness to eternal life. Their hope fills their eyes, and simplicity and love shine through every word and action. They fill their days with work, effective spiritual testimony, and prayer that speaks of the Holy Spirit's presence and glorifies God. They live joyfully and depart with crowns of gladness upon their heads, glorifying God in both their life and death.

Therefore, God is not unjust to confine us to these old, earthly bodies when before us stand those who have clearly transcended them and recovered their new creation stored in the heart — the very temple of God where His Spirit dwells. God awaits the end of ignorance, the passing of wasted time, and the onset of labour through prayer and tears, so that this new self can be revealed and accepted in us. Then, the promise will be fulfilled, and we will receive the covenant with our spirit, living in the fullness of the Gospel's truth according to God's plan, which He has created in us for His glory and for worship, thanksgiving, and joy. Indeed! This is the life God has bestowed upon us in our new spiritual creation, paid for by the sacrifice of His Son on the cross and His resurrection, so that we may live in Him and with Him in that same resurrection.

CHAPTER EIGHT.

ETERNAL LIFE UNVEILED:
FAITH, LOVE, AND THE NEW CREATION IN CHRIST

Faith in Christ and a Personal Relationship with Him

In Christian faith, the essence of a personal relationship with Christ stands as the most profound and vital cornerstone of a believer's life in Christ Jesus. Faith can either be confined to intellectual understanding, where Christ is perceived as a distant figure to be approached mentally — examined, discussed, and described as Jesus Christ, the Son of God, God incarnate, the Savior, and Redeemer. Such an understanding remains within the intellectual domain, reliant on cognitive recognition and memorization.

Alternatively, faith can be rooted in the testimony of the Spirit and the deep existential impression Christ makes on the new inner self. This inner transformation, marked by Christ's suffering on the cross and imbued with His resurrection power, brings about a living, vibrant presence of Christ within us. As Paul the Apostle proclaimed with certainty and public testimony, this mystical union with Christ is so profound that he could say, "*It is no longer I who live, but Christ lives in me*" (Gal.2:20). This reflects Christ's divine promise: "*You are in Me, and I am in you*" (John.14:20) and "*Abide in Me, and I in you*" (John.15:4).

This represents the reality of spiritual faith, distinct from mere intellectual knowledge of the Son of God. Faith in Christ operates on two levels:

Intellectual Understanding: This involves a rational grasp of God's nature, which can be extensively analysed and discussed, viewing Christ as a distant concept to be described and observed.

Spiritual Awareness: This is an intimate perception of the Spirit, where one experiences the Lord in a manner that transcends the self, finding one's true identity only in Him: *"For His sake I have lost all things; I consider them rubbish that I may gain Christ and be found in Him"* (Phil.3:8-9). Paul's writings and life show that he considered everything else as loss compared to the surpassing value of knowing Christ. For Paul, Christ filled his being so completely that he thought and felt nothing apart from Christ.

This spiritual awareness of Christ's all-encompassing presence cannot be fully grasped by the intellect alone, as the mind perceives only the external and not the essence of the self. Spiritual faith in Christ involves making Him one's very essence, where neither Christ nor oneself exists separately: *"But he who is joined to the Lord is one spirit with Him"* (1Cor.6:17). Consequently, nothing can separate us from the love of Christ, not even death or life (Rom.8:35-39).

Christ is the totality that fills everything: *"the fullness of Him who fills all in all"* (Eph.1:23). No individual can fully comprehend Christ except to the extent that they are filled by Him. The extent of understanding Christ depends on one's participation and union with Him. Christ reveals Himself to me according to the capacity of my faith and spiritual perception. Outside of this, Christ is perceived only intellectually as a separate entity. There is a significant difference between Christ revealing Himself to me and my intellectual understanding of

Him. Christ's self-revelation to me results from my faith and union with Him through His grace, while intellectual understanding remains external until I accept Him by faith, allowing the Spirit's revelation to deepen my comprehension.

Thus, faith in Christ embodies the truth of my relationship with Him and His relationship with me. Abiding in Christ and Christ abiding in me, as expressed in the union with Christ, represents the true and practical measure of faith: *"Our fellowship is with the Father and with His Son Jesus Christ"* (1 John.1:3).

Here, knowing Christ and believing in Him is a personal experience rather than an intellectual exercise: *"Unless you believe that I am He, you will die in your sins"* (John.8:24). Faith in Christ means believing in His very being as the *"I Am,"* a title from the Old Testament. This personal faith does not arise from intellectual understanding but from accepting Him as our new, true life, previously hidden with the Father and now revealed according to John's experiential testimony: *"That which we have seen with our eyes, which we have looked at and our hands have touched, this we proclaim concerning the Word of life... This is the message we have heard from Him and declare to you: God is light; in Him there is no darkness at all. If we claim to have fellowship with Him and yet walk in the darkness, we lie and do not live out the truth"* (1 John 1:1, 5-6).

The Revelation of Christ and the Promise of Eternal Life

In this passage, the Apostle John introduces a crucial theological insight: the revelation of the *"Word"* is essentially the revelation of eternal life that was once hidden with God the Father but has now been made manifest through Christ. John emphasizes the term "*to us*," highlighting that this revelation is specifically for us, much like the sun's light and warmth are for us. Christ's manifestation is thus intensely personal and particular, as John asserts that the eternal life with the Father has been "*revealed*" to us by divine will. This unique and profound revelation is what John describes as our "*fellowship*" with the Father and His Son, Jesus Christ.

This revelation inherently includes processes of selection, sanctification, and justification. John encapsulates all of Paul's teachings on redemption, salvation, reconciliation, justification, and adoption into one comprehensive act: the revelation of eternal life, which was with the Father and manifested through the Word specifically for us. This manifestation encompasses us, bringing us into eternal life, which exists in Christ and the Father, thus making us participants in divine life shared with the Father and the Son. This represents the ultimate fulfilment of salvation and aligns with the pinnacle of God's love and grace, as demonstrated to Paul, who, after his conversion and baptism, proclaimed Christ as the Son of God. Paul was enveloped by eternal life, living in communion with the Father and the Son without further instruction, knowing only that he was once blind but now sees.

This leads to the concept of complete joy, which is the result of eternal life flowing into us without expectation, suffering, or effort on our part. This reflects the free and generous nature of God's grace. Just as the blind man received full sight by mere will: "*Rabbi, I want to see*" (Mark.10:51), and received sight "*according to your faith*" (Matt.9:29), John does not diminish the importance of redemption and atonement. Instead, he describes them as securing the eternal life revealed in Jesus Christ, ensuring our continued fellowship in it. Jesus had previously declared Himself as the resurrection and the life: "*I am the resurrection and the life. The one who believes in Me will live, even though they die*" (John. 11:25). Martha affirmed this by saying: "*Yes, Lord, I believe that You are the Messiah, the Son of God, who is to come into the world*" (John.11:27), pointing to the revelation. Jesus had also declared Himself as the way, the truth, and the life before His crucifixion (John.14:6).

John views the cross, death, and atonement as affirming and securing the eternal life revealed to us through the Incarnation. According to this revelation, we are united in the Spirit with the Father and the Son, as John proclaimed: "*We proclaim to you what we have seen and heard, so that you also may have fellowship with us. And our fellowship is with the Father and with His Son, Jesus Christ. We write this to make our joy complete*" (1 John.1:3-4).

John considers the revelation of Jesus Christ, the Son of God, to be the fulfilment of God's promise: "*And this is what He promised us—eternal life*" (1 John.2:25). The manifestation of Christ as eternal life is proof of the Father's love: "*This is how God showed His love among us: He sent His one and only Son into the world that we might live through Him*" (1 John.4:9). The work of eternal life in us, which is the manifestation of God's love through Christ Jesus, precedes the work of atonement. God loved us first and then provided atonement for our sins through the death of His Son: "*This is love: not that we loved God, but that He loved us and sent His Son as an atoning sacrifice for our sins*" (1 John.4:10). Thus, atonement for sins ensures the realization of eternal life.

The second birth from water and the Spirit, or birth from God, is akin to entering eternal life where there is no sin: "*No one who is born of God will continue to sin, because God's seed remains in them; they cannot go on sinning, because they have been born of God"* (1 John.3:9). Sin is considered an act against God, as it originates from the devil: *"The one who does what is sinful is of the devil, because the devil has been sinning from the beginning"* (1 John 3:8). Christ came to destroy the devil's works: *"The reason the Son of God appeared was to destroy the devil's work"* (1 John.3:8). Hence, sin is defined as *"an act against God,"* stemming from the devil's work. Consequently, one born of God does not commit sin, as God's seed—the Spirit of life—within them cannot act against God. John further distinguishes between a mortal sin, which is unforgivable (1 John.5:16-17), such as denying Christ as the Son of God and rejecting the revelation of eternal life, and other sins which do not involve such denial. These can be forgiven through confession: *"If we confess our sins, He is faithful and just and will forgive us our sins and purify us from all unrighteousness"* (1 John 1:9). The blood of Jesus Christ, His Son, purifies us from all sin (1 John 1:7).

The Apostle John on Sin, Atonement, and Eternal Life

The Apostle John emphasizes that we should avoid sin, thus making it a matter of personal choice. However, he also reassures us that sin is covered by the power of Christ's atonement through His intercession with God the Father. John writes, *"My dear children, I write this to you so that you will not sin. But if anybody does sin, we have an advocate with the Father—Jesus Christ, the Righteous One. He is the atoning sacrifice for our sins, and not only for ours but also for the sins of the whole world"* (1 John.2:1-2). In this way, John ensures that our place in eternal life, in fellowship with the Father and His Son Jesus Christ, is secure. By placing sin under the authority of

Christ's intercession and forgiveness, our lives are safeguarded against death and destruction, ensuring instead that we remain steadfast in Christ with complete joy.

For John, eternal life is the theological equivalent of salvation as described by Paul. Whereas Paul focuses on salvation's culmination through atonement, redemption, reconciliation, and adoption, John begins and ends with eternal life. This perspective is evident in his Gospel, which starts with the concept of eternal life: *"In Him was life, and that life was the light of all mankind"* (John 1:4), and concludes by stating that the purpose of the Gospel is to grant us life through His name: *"But these are written that you may believe that Jesus is the Messiah, the Son of God, and that by believing you may have life in His name"* (John.20:31). Similarly, John's first letter begins with eternal life: *"The life appeared; we have seen it and testify to it, and we proclaim to you the eternal life, which was with the Father and has appeared to us"* (1 John.1:2), and concludes by affirming eternal life: *"We know also that the Son of God has come and has given us understanding, so that we may know Him who is true. And we are in Him who is true—by being in His Son Jesus Christ. He is the true God and eternal life"* (1 John 5:20).

John affirms that eternal life is granted through faith in Jesus Christ. Christ ensures our participation in this eternal life through His intercession with the Father, having offered Himself as the atoning sacrifice for our sins and for the sins of the entire world. Thus, John reassures his readers that their sins are forgiven, enabling them to live with a *"clear conscience"* in line with Paul's message in Hebrews: *"How much more will the blood of Christ, who through the eternal Spirit offered Himself unblemished to God, cleanse our consciences from acts that lead to death, so that we may serve the living God!"* (Heb.9:14).

John fortifies our consciences with a sure promise of forgiveness through Christ: "*If we confess our sins, He is faithful and just and will forgive us our sins and purify us from all unrighteousness*" (1 John.1:9). This recurring emphasis on reducing guilt and enhancing our enjoyment of fellowship with the Father and the Son is vital for completing our joy. For John, experiencing salvation is akin to enjoying eternal life and fellowship with the Father and the Son. While faith guards salvation according to Paul, love is the protector of eternal life and fellowship with the Father and the Son according to John. Where Paul views sin as nullified by grace, John sees it overcome by love. Salvation, for Paul, is a journey from earth to heaven and from humanity to God. In contrast, John presents eternal life as a divine revelation that immerses us, allowing us to experience fellowship with the Father and the Son, with our response being: "*I was blind but now I see*" (John.9:25).

Eternal life, for John, is characterized by two elements of the Spirit: knowledge and love. "*Knowledge*" is the result of revelation because the revelation of the Word that was with the Father and has been made manifest to us immediately leads to knowing the Father, and knowing the Father generates love: "*I no longer call you servants, because a servant does not know his master's business. Instead, I have called you friends, for everything that I learned from My Father I have made known to you*" (John.15:15).

Thus, the essence of eternal life for John is "*love and knowledge*," with knowledge also being described in terms of light and truth. John delights in associating love with light: "*Anyone who loves their brother and sister lives in the light, and there is nothing in them to make them stumble. But anyone who hates a brother or sister is in the darkness and walks around in the darkness; they do not know where they are going, because the darkness has blinded them"* (1 John.2:10-11). If light represents God and truth, John's objective becomes clear: those who love remain in God and truth, while those who hate are outside of God, in darkness, where there is no path, door, or vision.

Moreover, *"Everyone who loves has been born of God"* (1 John.4:7), because Christian love is a characteristic of the new creation, born in the image of God. Therefore, love becomes a sensitive measure of the new birth, that is, the new creation through the Spirit.

Love, Knowledge, and Revelation: Understanding Eternal Life

John teaches us that love is rooted in knowledge, and knowledge arises from revelation. This suggests that the love we extend to others is a form of revelatory love. But what does this mean? It means that loving my brother involves discovering a divine truth that draws me toward him, creating a mutual attraction directed toward God and enriched by new divine understanding. This confirms that our love is grounded in light and sustained by it. Such love is described as being in God, in Christ, in the Spirit, in truth, in light, and in eternal life.

Love is life, and life is an experience of love shared with others. Thus, hatred represents death and destruction—it causes death to both my own soul and that of my brother, as hatred deprives us of life: *"Anyone who hates a brother or sister is a murderer"* (1 John 3:15).

There is a profound difference between physical love and spiritual love. Physical love involves a connection between individuals that ultimately leads to death, whereas spiritual love connects souls with

Christ, representing eternal life and unity. This transformation occurred when eternal life, which was with the Father, was revealed, bringing a love that unites those who accept it. This established fellowship with God and His Son Jesus Christ, resulting in complete joy.

The revelation of eternal life also brought about a revelation of fellowship with the Father and His Son Jesus Christ. This involved the Father's love that unites and the light (knowledge of the Father) that brings unity. The direct result of the Father revealing Himself through the Son is illustrated by Jesus' words: *"I have made You known to them, and will continue to make You known in order that the love You have for Me may be in them and that I Myself may be in them"* (John.17:26). Jesus also prayed, *"That all of them may be one, Father, just as You are in Me and I am in You. May they also be in Us so that the world may believe that You have sent Me"* (John.17:21).

This *"revelation"* brought by the Son from the Father—knowledge of the Father and the Father's love poured into the Son—is the fellowship John speaks of, which they had with the Father and His Son Jesus Christ, and it is the secret of complete joy. Christ presented this to the apostles, who shared it with the same love, light, and knowledge, so we could participate in fellowship with the Father and the Son. This was Christ's request from the Father at the end of His earthly life: *"That the love You have for Me may be in them and that I Myself may be in them"* (John.17:26). When the Father's love for the Son is poured into us and the Son is in us, we inevitably and necessarily become united with the Father and His Son Jesus Christ.

Thus, the mystery John expresses: *"Dear friends, now we are children of God, and what we will be has not yet been made known. But we know that when Christ appears, we shall be like Him, for we shall see*

Him as He is" (1 John.3:2). If the Father's love for the Son has become part of us, and if Christ the Son is in us, what more is needed to make us like Him? If He is in us and the Father's love for the Son is in us, we have become like Him. Although it is challenging to imagine this in our current physical state, in the new creation, when Christ is revealed, we will indeed be like Him because we will see Him as He is in us!

This is not a mere assertion by John; the Son Himself took on our form and became like us in the flesh, using the opportunity to transform our form into His through the Spirit—creating a new spiritual humanity in the image of God: "*Put on the new self, created to be like God in true righteousness and holiness*" (Eph.4:24) and "*Put on the new self, which is being renewed in knowledge in the image of its Creator*" (Col.3:10). Thus, ultimately, we will "*be like Him, because we will see Him as He is in us.*"

Paul addresses this concept in stages. He explains, "*Put on the new self, created to be like God in true righteousness and holiness*" (Eph.4:24), referring to the second birth of water and the Spirit, known as being "*born from above*" for those "*born of God.*" This confirms that through our baptism, we now embody the new self, regarded as a new spiritual creation according to God, "*in true righteousness and holiness,*" which are essential qualities for unity or fellowship with the Creator. Paul further confirms that this new self or spiritual creation within us is renewed in knowledge—i.e., the revelation of God the Father—to be in the image of its Creator, preparing us for fellowship with the Father and the Son.

The Overlooked Truth:
Embracing Our New Creation in Christ

This profound truth has regrettably been neglected by many theologians and scholars. It is astonishing that we might undervalue the tremendous work of God, which clothes us with the new self-created in His image, in righteousness and holiness, granting us the privilege of free fellowship with God the Father and His Son Jesus Christ. If we confine ourselves to our physical existence and neglect the new spiritual creation we received through baptism and the breath of the Holy Spirit—created in the image of God and Christ, marked by righteousness and holiness—then we become the most wretched of creatures, and Christ's sacrifice on our behalf would seem in vain.

The peril of disregarding the gifts of our new creation is that it deprives us of genuine fellowship with the Father and the Son Jesus Christ. Without the new self within us, a true relationship with Christ—and therefore with the Father—is impossible. Christian faith does not emanate from the old, physical self, as it is incapable of such faith. As the Apostle Paul writes: "*If you declare with your mouth, 'Jesus is Lord,' and believe in your heart that God raised Him from the dead, you will be saved*" (Rom.10:9). What does it mean to "*believe in your heart*"? The heart is the centre of truth, sincerity, and honour in a person, attributes belonging not to the physical self but to the spiritual self.

Faith is the work of the new self because faith in Christ is unrelated to the earthly man. The new creation, fashioned in Christ's image, expresses its faith, love, and connection to Christ, making its faith genuine and real. Confession with the mouth pertains to the senses: "*That which was from the beginning, which we have heard, which we have seen with our eyes, which we have looked at and our hands have touched — this we proclaim concerning the Word of life"* (1 John.1:1). Thus, confession with the mouth involves the senses and intellect.

What is crucial is that Christian faith originates from the new self- created in the image of God in holiness and truth. Therefore, faith is considered a significant and vital act: *"Did I not tell you that if you believe, you will see the glory of God?"* (John.11:40). When we correctly place faith in Christ as an expression of the new self- born of God in holiness and truth — demonstrating love, intimacy, union, and fellowship — this becomes the true faith that imparts eternal life. It reflects living in eternal life within fellowship with the Father and His Son Jesus Christ, where we experience complete joy. This joy is currently lost to us due to a misunderstanding of our faith in Christ, which has been limited to intellectual acknowledgment of the Son's divine attributes without real spiritual sensation or sincere love.

The result of a flawed faith in Christ, based on the perception of the new self- born of God, is that we continue to feel like sinners and perceive ourselves as estranged from God and Christ. The key characteristic of the new self- born of God is that it does not sin: *"We know that anyone born of God does not sin; the One born of God keeps them safe, and the evil one cannot harm them. We know that we are children of God, and that the whole world is under the control of the evil one. We know also that the Son of God has come and has given us understanding, so that we may know Him who is true. And we are in Him who is true — by being in His Son Jesus Christ. He is the true God and eternal life"* (1 John.5:18-20). We have lost the sense of being born of God, clothed in Christ's righteousness, protected from the evil one, and possessing the insight to know the truth and live in eternal life in Christ Jesus. This is due to a misunderstanding that faith in Christ is the work of the new self- born of the Spirit, and that true faith is a state of love and connection with Christ, not merely an intellectual concept we articulate with our mouths while our spiritual awareness and the reality of Christ are absent.

John's statement at the end of the fifth chapter, *"We know that anyone born of God does not sin; but the One born of God keeps them safe, and the evil one cannot harm them"* (1 John.5:18), reflects the state of the new self in us, as it is a new creation in the image of God in holiness and truth. Another verse says, *"No one who is born of God will continue to sin, because God's seed remains in them; they cannot go on sinning, because they have been born of God"* (1 John.3:9). Sin has become an act of the old self, the body of death, and even this can be forgiven through confession. However, John emphasizes that the one born of God does not sin, nor can they sin because they are born of God—meaning they are immersed in God, with God's seed (His Spirit) within them, as well as His Word (Christ): *"If Christ is in you, then even though your body is subject to death because of sin, the Spirit gives life because of righteousness"* (Rom.8:10). Paul's statement, *"The righteous will live by faith"* (Rom.1:17), is of significant importance to John, as the righteous are those who have received Christ's righteousness through faith in His death and resurrection. As Paul elaborates, "For it is with your heart that you believe and are justified, and it is with your mouth that you profess your faith and are saved" (Rom.10:10). Belief in Christ's resurrection grants us Christ's righteousness: *"He was delivered over to death for our sins and was raised to life for our justification"* (Rom.4:25). Christ's death, in which we died with Him, removed the curse of death, and His resurrection granted us His righteousness, as He obeyed His Father unto death on our behalf.

Thus, the righteous are those who believe in Christ's resurrection and live with Him in His righteousness, representing fellowship according to John. Fellowship with the Father and His Son Jesus Christ is the source of complete Christian joy. For Paul, living in righteousness by faith is fellowship with the Father and the Son according to John. Interestingly, while faith is the primary catalyst for righteous living in Paul's writings, John identifies the source of eternal life's fellowship as divine revelation: "*The life appeared; we have seen it and testify to it, and we proclaim to you the eternal life, which was with the Father and has appeared to us*" (1 John.1:2). God appeared in the flesh and freely gave us eternal life!

In Paul's view, everyone who believes becomes a child of God (Gal.3:26). For John, "*Everyone who loves has been born of God*" (1 John.4:7). But there is no difference—those who believe do so from their new self-born of God, and those who love do so from their new self-born of God. John's contribution is that love has the power of faith. Thus, faith is an act of love. My faith in Christ means I am turning toward Him and holding onto His love. By loving Christ, I demonstrate that I am truly a child of God, for "*Everyone who loves has been born of God*" (1 John.4:7). "*The Father Himself loves you because you have loved Me*" (John.16:27). "*Anyone who loves Me will be loved by My Father, and I too will love them and show Myself to them*" (John 14:21). Here, love in John's writings takes the place of faith in Paul's writings. Therefore, a mere profession of faith in Christ is insufficient—love is essential: "*Simon son of John, do you love Me? ... Feed My sheep*" (John.21:17). Ultimately, as stated at the beginning of this chapter, faith in Christ necessitates a personal relationship with Him. So, are you truly a believer in Christ?

Chapter Nine.

Standing Before God:
The New Creation Through Worship and Prayer.

Standing Before God:
The Essence of the New Creation

The verse "*He chose us in Him before the foundation of the world to be holy and blameless before Him in love*" (Eph.1:4) marks both the beginning and the culmination of our understanding of the new creation. This verse reveals that the ultimate purpose of the new creation is to be prepared to stand before God. But what does this standing truly entail?

The first part of the verse speaks of being "*holy and blameless before Him in love.*" This is not a condition but an intrinsic aspect of our new creation, designed according to God's eternal plan. It is God's will that humanity should be "*holy and blameless in love*" as part of our fundamental design, enabling us to stand before Him — not through effort, but as a gift ingrained in our new nature.

The Apostle Paul made this truth clear to the Gentiles who believed in Christ, stating that they have received this new nature through Christ's work: "*Once you were alienated from God and were enemies in your minds because of your evil behaviour. But now He has reconciled you by Christ's physical body through death to present you holy in His sight, without blemish and free from accusation — if you continue in your faith, established and firm, and do not move from the hope held out in the gospel*" (Col.1:21-23). Thus, this new state is a gift from Christ. Having received this new creation—part of God's eternal plan before the world was founded—through the rebirth of water and Spirit, we are called to experience this state when standing before God. This experience often transcends our current weak reality due to the old self's weight pressing down on the new spiritual self within us. Yet, in moments of spiritual warmth, we may briefly taste this state, as a foretaste of what we will fully experience when the old self and time are removed.

Nevertheless, this state does not originate from us. It is the gifts bestowed upon the new spiritual self during prayer, as these gifts are the result of Christ's grace working within us. Our nearness to God or our approach is fundamentally due to the truth that "*the Lord is near*" humanity! The person who has believed, been baptized, and accepted their new creation in the second birth has put on Christ, as Paul explains: "*For all of you who were baptized into Christ have clothed yourselves with Christ*" (Gal.3:27). Consequently, they have received what belongs to Christ: "*For in Christ all the fullness of the Deity lives in bodily form, and in Christ you have been brought to fullness*" (Col.2:9-10).

While standing before God is the on-going state of the new self, and represents Christ's grace enabling us to be near God and stand before Him in holiness and blamelessness in love, this state initially occupies only a fleeting moment. It is not a result of experience, merit, or worthiness, and does not begin with us—even if we stand before Him for hours. The approach to God is initiated by Him, as He is the source of the qualification that allows us to stand before Him in holiness and blamelessness in love. God reveals Himself as the Father, and we draw from Him the Spirit of son-ship, standing in holiness and blamelessness in love, enveloped by His power like a cloud covering the disciples during the Transfiguration.

However, this experience is momentary, and we often revert to a state of weakness, where holiness and blamelessness in love become distant aspirations. God's initiative in nearness — *"the Lord is near"* — and His revelation as Father is only for a moment. We feel close to Him and attain the state of son-ship and holiness in love momentarily. Without being hidden in Christ, we could not be near or stand before God. In our approach to God, Christ acts as the hand that covers God's face so we do not see Him directly. Through Christ, we perceive behind Him, which is His glory (Exod.33:18-23): *"And we all, who with unveiled faces contemplate the Lord's glory, are being transformed into His image with ever-increasing glory, which comes from the Lord, who is the Spirit"* (2 Cor.3:18). This is sufficient because: *"Anyone who has seen Me has seen the Father"* (John.14:9).

In standing before God, while hidden in Christ, we receive what is needed to strengthen our new self, rejuvenate its faculties, and sustain its existence amidst worldly challenges, the burden of the old body, and its distractions. These are days of pilgrimage, not settlement, where prayer sustains our journey. Additionally, we receive a heavenly calling from Christ that renews our hope, increasing our desire and boldness to stand before God and draw nearer. This invitation comes from Christ's words: *"God is spirit, and His worshipers must worship in the Spirit and in truth... for they are the kind of worshipers the Father seeks"* (John.4:23-24). This is a treasure we add to the potential and capabilities that God has implanted in the new self, enabling us to stand before God in holiness and blamelessness in love.

The Divine Invitation: Worshiping God in Spirit and Truth

When Christ reveals that God seeks worshipers in spirit and truth, we understand that this invitation is a divine decree from God Himself. It signifies a formal, personal request from God, transforming our approach to Him in prayer and worship from mere longing to an official mandate. This call is not just for standing before God but also for entering His presence and worshiping Him in spirit and truth. By emphasizing that God desires worshipers who engage "*in spirit and truth,*" Christ highlights a profound calling for the new creation in Christ to consciously fulfil this divine relationship as an imperative, exceeding mere instruction — it's a sacred demand.

Thus, when we approach God in prayer and stand before Him, we are responding to a high calling rather than presuming. Our approach is a fulfilment of God's demand to come near and worship Him in spirit and truth. This involves the new creation He has made for us in Christ, allowing us to approach Him with confidence and assurance of acceptance, given to us in a state of holiness and blamelessness in love. Our presence before Him is a result of our union in Christ, experiencing adoption and completing God's will — a paternal request we fulfil as children through Christ.

What stands out is why God desires worshipers in spirit and truth. This is the first time we hear God asking something specifically for Himself. The answer is provided by the Apostle Paul: "*He predestined us for adoption to son-ship through Jesus Christ, in accordance with His pleasure and will*" (Eph.1:5). God's earnest desire for us to appear as His children reflects "*His pleasure*" or delight. This delight reaches its height when we hear that God seeks such children to worship Him in spirit and truth—a request that is truly astonishing. The majestic God, before whom countless angels worship and praise, overlooks this grand display to look upon humanity, whose hearts find rest in Him, calling them to appear before Him to worship in spirit and truth for His own pleasure. This is truly remarkable!

We grasp from this how and why God envelops us in holiness and removes all blame in love so we can approach Him and stand before Him. This is to fulfil His pleasure in us! This realization brings profound peace, as we ponder how we could attain holiness and blamelessness in love to stand before God. But God, who understands our needs and our earthly state, has embedded this *"holiness and blamelessness in love"* in the very fabric of His original creation of humanity, as Paul writes: *"created to be like God in true righteousness and holiness"* (Eph.4:24). This divine nature enables us to stand proudly before the angels of God. This understanding compels us to reassess our concept of prayer, drawing near to God, appearing before Him, and worshiping Him in spirit and truth with our new selves. We discover that it is God's pleasure, and He Himself is the one calling and demanding this for His own sake.

Therefore, approaching God, appearing before Him, and worshiping Him in spirit and truth become urgent acts for God's sake and His delight. This is not merely for moments but should be the focus of our entire lives, as this pleases God's heart! Our hours and prayers become acts of fulfilling God's pleasure, as we, His children, return to His embrace, bringing joy to both Him and ourselves. As it is written, *"Let the children come to Me and do not hinder them... for their angels in heaven always see the face of My Father in heaven"* (Matt.18:10; 19:14).

Our hesitations to draw near to God — whether due to fear, self-consciousness, or misguided feelings of unworthiness — are excuses that do not reflect God's intentions or His transformative work within us. Rather, they are distractions from the old self, which masks itself with deceit to avoid facing God. In contrast, the new self within us is eager to seek God's presence. Missing from God's sight is like a child who has strayed, signifying a withdrawal from the love of the Father and a failure to recognize the Father's deep desire for the child's return.

This illustrates the profound suitability of our new creation for standing before God, as described in Ephesians 4:24: *"created to be like God in true righteousness and holiness."* This new creation is inherently equipped to stand before God and worship Him in spirit and truth. It embodies the potential for holiness and blamelessness in love, ensuring we are always prepared to offer praise and glorify God's grace, which He has abundantly given to us in the Beloved, fulfilling His divine will.

We come to understand why the soul finds such profound joy and peace when it starts to connect with the practice of prayer. The joy felt in standing before God and worshiping Him grows deeper with each moment of prayer and continued presence. This joy, stemming from God's will, resonates back to us, filling our souls with the Father's delight, even when we feel we have nothing to offer or no merit of our own. This overwhelming happiness is a direct result of the divine will, embracing our souls with paternal love.

In essence, the new creation in Christ Jesus is spiritually designed to maintain constant communion with God. We experience a glimpse of this eternal relationship through our acts of worship and prayer, serving as a preview of true fellowship with the Father and His Son, Jesus Christ. This is practiced through our daily prayers and acts of worship, which are a foretaste of the deep and abiding connection we are meant to enjoy with God.

The Divine Urgency of Prayer: Christ's Example and God's Love Revealed

This insight unveils why Christ emphasized the necessity of prayer, exemplified by His own practice of praying on the mountain throughout the night. For Christ, the concept of *"moment"* in prayer is illustrated by His *"all-night prayers,"* highlighting the immense potential afforded to us. When Christ instructed us to "pray always," *He meant to turn every moment into an opportunity to stand before God. His command to "pray and not lose heart"* (Luke.18:1) encourages us to weave these moments together to savour the full richness of communion and its blessings. His teaching on persistent prayer reveals the boldness needed to seek God's response, while His discourse on praying with fervour shows the intensity of the spirit when it exceeds its limits.

Through these examples, Christ painted vivid images of the human soul meeting God, striving to overcome personal barriers to remain in His presence despite obstacles. This process completes not only our joy but, more significantly, the joy of God Himself, fulfilling our communion with the Father and His Son, Jesus Christ.

The phrase *"in love"* in the latter part of the verse reveals that God has embedded His most precious element within the core of our creation. This divine element draws us to God and binds us to Him in ways beyond our full comprehension. Thus, our approach to God is *"in love."* Holiness and blamelessness are encompassed within this divine love embedded in the nature of the new creation as a spiritual instinct. We are deeply grateful to God for this wondrous grace—instilling divine love into the nature of humanity created in righteousness and holiness. This divine love operates within us through a divine impulse from God, not merely as human effort. The spiritual person, when approaching God, is naturally inclined towards Him with an inner love that acts independently of conscious effort, marked by clear signs such as a fervent heart during prayer, often resulting in tears and cries from an inexplicable source. This is the divine love embedded in the heart, expressing itself through powerful reactions to the Father's revelation of His love when the son's love meets the Father's love unobstructed.

This moment of divine encounter and presence before God is captured in 1 John 4:9-10: "*This is how God showed His love among us: He sent His one and only Son into the world that we might live through Him. This is love: not that we loved God, but that He loved us and sent His Son as an atoning sacrifice for our sins.*"

We can be assured that our approach to God, our standing before Him, and our worship and love are not purely our own initiative. Such an endeavour would be impossible for us, given our experiences of the struggle to pray and worship when the spirit is weak and the old self resists. However, when the new creation within us awakens and begins to operate, the dread of approaching God vanishes, and the avoidance of prayer ceases abruptly, replaced by a strong inclination towards prayer as if driven by a powerful force. This is the divine love within us.

If someone is absent from prayer due to unavoidable circumstances, they may feel an inner call—this is the divine love within us—drawing them back to God. Upon returning to stand before God, it feels as though He was waiting for them, leading to a heartfelt resumption of prayer and worship, akin to a child reuniting with their Father after a period of absence.

From this, it becomes clear that the divine love embedded in the new nature of humanity is central to our relationship with God. When this divine element is overshadowed by the old self, standing before God for prayer or worship becomes a struggle fraught with conflict, leading to excuses and evasion of God's presence. Thus, divine love is revealed as the core element God implanted in our new nature, designed to sustain our eternal relationship with Him in perpetual worship and everlasting love. Christ offers a profound vision of this paternal love binding us to God: *"Righteous Father, though the world does not know you, I know you, and they know that you have sent me. I have made you known to them, and will continue to make you known in order that the love you have for me may be in them and that I myself may be in them"* (John.17:25-26). This is beyond human comprehension—God the Father sharing with us the love He has for the Son, the most sacred aspect of the relationship between Father and Son.

The Sanctity of Love and the Requirements for Standing Before God

We have emphasized the element of *"love"* over the phrase *"holy and blameless"* because its significance and practical implications demand it. To be *"holy and blameless"* without love does not qualify one to approach or stand before God. Love serves as the magnetic force that draws and moves the human soul towards its beloved. Thus, *"holiness and blamelessness"* are qualities that follow from love: *"holy and blameless... in love."*

The essence of holy love is its exclusive devotion to God. Christ taught that love must be wholly directed towards God—sacred and undivided—meaning that the heart, soul, and mind should love no one or nothing else but God. In this pure devotion, worldly and bodily desires fade away, and inclinations towards others are extinguished. Moreover, distracting thoughts and imaginations are replaced by a focus solely on God. Thus, love is sanctified in heart, soul, and mind, enabling one to stand before God as a cherished child.

The term "*blameless*" pertains to the conscience, which serves as an internal witness to God's law and an overseer of one's actions and behaviours. The conscience determines whether one can stand before God to pray and worship. When all sources of blame are removed and replaced with encouragement, a person is free to approach God in prayer without internal barriers.

However, from human experience, no matter how revered or holy one may be, no one is entirely free from a blameworthy conscience. Every saint, regardless of their holiness, ultimately acknowledges their unworthiness to stand before God without fault. Yet Christ bore all human sins and shortcomings, offering Himself as a sacrifice to purify humanity's soul, body, and spirit. He cleansed the human conscience from all blame and dead works (Heb.9:14), making us "*created in God's image in righteousness and holiness of truth,*" where righteousness means removing all blame, for the righteous are undoubtedly blameless before God.

Thus, in our new creation, the blame from the conscience and the law is removed forever, allowing us to stand before God without anxiety, practicing love, prayer, and closeness. Instead of blame, God has instilled in us the confidence and His paternal love.

Standing before God is one of the most daunting tasks granted to humanity, as the awe of God's presence shakes the very essence of a person and any spiritual being, no matter their stature. Isaiah's vision vividly illustrates the profound experience of being before God:

"In the year that King Uzziah died, I saw the Lord sitting on a high and lofty throne, and the hem of His robe filled the temple. Seraphim were standing above Him; each one had six wings: with two he covered his face, with two he covered his feet, and with two he flew. And one called to another: 'Holy, holy, holy is the Lord of Hosts; His glory fills the whole earth.' The foundations of the doorway shook at the sound of their voices, and the temple was filled with smoke. Then I said: 'Woe is me, for I am ruined, because I am a man of unclean lips and live among a people of unclean lips, and because my eyes have seen the King, the Lord of Hosts'" (Isa.6:1-5).

Given Isaiah's experience, who would approach God's presence lightly? Yet, God created humanity with inherent holiness and blamelessness in love, preparing them to stand before Him. Christ declared that God, based on the qualifications of the new nature He bestowed upon humanity, seeks worshippers who worship in spirit and truth. Thus, God has qualified us with holiness and blamelessness in love to stand before Him. He has removed the terror of His presence, allowing us to approach Him and express our love and emotions as children to a Father. Simultaneously, God's will is fulfilled in the joy of human son-ship through Christ. Our experience of exercising filial confidence before God in prayer, when filled with love, dispels all fear or apprehension of His presence. When absent from prayer, we feel a strong desire to return and be before

Him, driven by the longing for love that finds its fulfilment in His presence. When the new creation within us is active, we are often impelled by sudden fervor to stand before God in prayer, sometimes repeatedly within the hour, never reaching a state of satisfaction.

It is evident that the new man experiences a profound sense of alienation from God, driven by the constraints of time in this present world and the old flesh that obstructs the spirit and diminishes the fervour of love. Yet, amidst this struggle, God continually graces us with moments of standing before Him in prayer and worship in spirit and truth, allowing us to draw deeply from His boundless love. These moments provide a profound compensation that helps us transcend the pain of our estrangement.

If we were to distil the essence of the new creation into a single word that encapsulates everything we have explored, it would be *"resurrection."* We have died with Christ through our sins and shared in the curse on the cross. This completed the penalty for everyone who believes in Christ. In His resurrection, we were brought to life, and the penalties of death and curse were removed. Through His resurrected body, we received the new human body, enabling us to live with Christ before God for eternity. The new creation is a resurrection body: *"If you have been raised with Christ, seek the things that are above..."* (Col.3:1) and *"He raised us up with Him and seated us with Him in the heavenly places..."* (Ephesians 2:6) and *"Even when we were dead in our trespasses, made us alive together with Christ."* (Eph.2:5)

The Pinnacle of the New Creation Intended by God for Humanity

It is no coincidence that our new creation in the new man reaches its culmination in a singular image — the image of our Creator. As it is written: "*You have taken off your old self with its practices and have put on the new self, which is being renewed in knowledge in the image of its Creator. Here there is no Greek or Jew, circumcised or uncircumcised, barbarian, Scythian, slave or free, but Christ is all, and is in all*" (Col.3:9-11). The Spirit has empowered humanity to attain this very image: "*And we all, who with unveiled faces contemplate the Lord's glory, are being transformed into his image with ever-increasing glory, which comes from the Lord, who is the Spirit*" (2 Cor.3:18).

Although the new man is created in the image of Christ — being of His flesh and bones — the new creation is given the potential to fully reflect the Creator's image in glory, as it is created to be exactly like Him. Thus, it is granted the opportunity to reach the fullness of Christ. The verse indicates that spiritual contemplation, firmly fixed on Christ with sincerity and strength, can elevate us from glory to glory, provided that it is without the veil of the law, commandments, dead traditions, and human heritage. This transformation is accomplished by the Spirit, who is the Lord of glory.

Additionally, growth toward the head of the new creation and its image is described as the work of genuine love: "*Instead, speaking the truth in love, we will grow to become in every respect the mature body of him who is the head, that is, Christ"* (Eph.4:15).

If each of us bears the image of Christ, where does hatred come from? Where do disputes and divisions arise, which are the weapons of the devil inherited from the old man allied with Satan? If Christ's image is truly *"the glory of God,"* then every image of Him must radiate with love. Each of us sees our brother as the ideal we aspire to become. Thus, through this elevation in the Lord's glory, we grow closer, more affectionate, and unified. This is the work of the new man created in the singular image of God's glory in the face of Jesus Christ. The ultimate aim of the new man, created in this unique image, is inevitably towards unity, driven by the allure of love and beauty in the face of Christ, whom we resemble in every aspect, as the Apostle John says: *"And now, dear children, continue in him, so that when he appears we may be confident and unashamed before him at his coming. If you know that he is righteous, you know that everyone who does what is right has been born of him. See what great love the Father has lavished on us, that we should be called children of God!... Dear friends, now we are children of God, and what we will be has not yet been made known. But we know that when Christ appears, we shall be like him, for we shall see him as he is!"* (1 John.2:28-29; 3:1).

Thus, we arrive at the pinnacle of the new man and God's purpose for him, as articulated by the Apostle Paul: *"For all of you who were baptized into Christ have clothed yourselves with Christ. There is neither Jew nor Gentile, neither slave nor free, nor is there male and female, for you are all one in Christ Jesus"* (Gal.3:27-28), and *"until we all reach unity in the faith and in the knowledge of the Son of God and become mature, attaining to the whole measure of the fullness of Christ"* (Eph.4:13). Through Christ, humanity is restored to its complete unity in the new and perfect image of God, which had been fragmented in Adam due to disobedience and sin. Here, we find stability and reliance on God's equal love, demonstrated through the Son's sacrifice, enabling humanity to finally unite in paternal love, measured by Christ: "*I will make known to them, so that the love you have for me may be in them and that I myself may be in them*" (John.17:26).

May the Lord grant us the profound understanding of this new creation, not just to comprehend it but to deeply internalize its truth, as it represents our entire life. This is what the Apostle Paul summarized: "*I have been crucified with Christ and I no longer live, but Christ lives in me. The life I now live in the body, I live by faith in the Son of God, who loved me and gave himself for me*" (Gal.2:20).

LOGOS ECHOES
WHEREVER LOGOS INSPIRE

Welcome To The Realm Of Logos

Where the profound realms of theology and spirituality intertwine, your journey of faith begins. Embark on a transformative quest for knowledge and spiritual growth as we offer a rich tapestry of E-books designed to nourish your soul and ignite your mind.

At the heart of Logos Echoes beats a passion for sharing the life-changing power of God's Word. We illuminate the timeless truths of Christianity with a fresh perspective, providing a captivating blend of deep theological insights and practical wisdom. By understanding the heart of God and the mind of Christ, we empower believers to live out their faith with confidence and purpose.

Our ministry is to ignite a flame within your heart, deepening your connection with Christ and equipping you to share His love with the world. Discover thought-provoking insights, practical guidance, and timeless truths that will transform your life, Through the life-changing message of Jesus Christ.

Together, we will unlock the boundless potential of your faith and experience the profound peace and fulfilment found in a deep relationship with Christ.

Waiting To Hear From You

If you find it worth it, please don't hesitate to contact us. Your feedback is like gold to us! These insights help us improve, grow, and create better Christian content for everyone. Share your thoughts and ideas with us. You are always welcome. And remember, our goal is:

**TOGETHER WITH LOGOS,
WE MAKE THE WORLD BETTER**

Email us: logosechoes@gmail.com

About the Author

Sameh Saied is A Researcher and Self-Published Author in the Field of Christian Studies, Particularly Focusing on the History of Early Christianity ,also the Founder of Logos Echoes Publications. His Aim is to Publish Works that address Theological, Biblical, and Spiritual Topics of interest to readers, to foster a deeper understanding of the Christian Faith, which is reflected in individual lives and society as a whole, by presenting diverse perspectives on the Bible and Christian Doctrines. Until now published four books:

- God Among Us: The Rational Case for the Incarnation.

- The Heart of Jesus: Unveiling His Eternal Love for Humanity.

- Restoring the Divine Participation: The Holy Spirit's Role and the Path to True Repentance.

- Recreating Humanity: Illuminating Our Divine Identity in Christ.